Art Center College Library
1700 Lida St.
Pasadena, CA 91103

ART CENTER COLLEGE OF DESIGN
3 3220 00222 0890

>the way of the SNOWBOARDER

DISCARD

>the way of the SNOWBOARDER

796.939
R325
2005

ROB REED

Art Center College Library
1700 Lida St.
Pasadena, CA 91103

HARRY N. ABRAMS, INC., PUBLISHERS

CONTENTS<

Art Center College Library
1700 Lida St.
Pasadena, CA 91103

// **PREVIOUS SPREAD:** Heikki Sorsa grabs a handful of his toe-side rail in Hemsedal, Norway, 2002. // **OPPOSITE:** Kier Dillon, Chile.

>INTRODUCTION: **SURFING MOUNTAINS**

Who invented snowboarding? The question is a loaded one, and the pursuit of an answer has been fueled mostly by the media's desire to put a face on the supposed father of snowboarding—to attribute what would be a tremendous accomplishment to one individual. The reality, however, is not that simple. Unlike the printing press or the light bulb, the birth of snowboarding did not happen in a single, defining breakthrough.

On the most fundamental level, snowboarding can be defined as sliding down a snow-covered hill on a single plank, standing sideways. Seen in this way, snowboarding's roots extend back to the early 1900s.

As far as we know, Mr. Vern Wicklund (1904–1993) was the first to fashion a purpose-built snowboard around 1917, in the town of Cloquet, Minnesota. Inspired by necessity, Wicklund sought a cheap alternative to skis. As his son Gordon Wicklund recalls, "[My father] always told me that the Finnish kids had skis, but he and his brothers and sisters didn't have anything, so they came up with barrel stave boards" (*The Snowboard Journal*, 2004)—in other words, snowboards made from recycled barrel wood, which had been used to deliver and store food. The key element was that the pieces of wood were curved so they'd float above the snow as opposed to plowing it. Wicklund then fit the nose with a rope for balance, a leather strap in the rear to keep his foot in place, and grooved rubber pieces under his feet for traction. Lastly, he carried a stick in his free hand to act as a rudder for carving turns. This last detail is essential, for carving is what separates merely standing up on a sled and sliding out of control from what we recognize as the sport of snowboarding.

In 1939 Wicklund and two partners went so far as to patent the idea. "Our invention relates to improvements in sleds and the like," the patent describes, "and has for one object to provide a new and improved type of sled which may be used for coasting or as a substitute for skis in jumping on snow or snow covered ground." This textual how-to corresponds to black-and-white home-video footage from that same time period showing their early attempts at developing technique. "My dad rode the boards into his fifties," Gordon remembers. "In the early '60s they thought about making the boards out of plastic, because plastic was getting popular at the time and they could've made them less expensively than with wood. I heard them talking about it, but they never got around to it." A few short years later, though, a man named Sherman Poppen did.

Widely considered the grandfather of modern snowboarding, Poppen brought the world the Snurfer, a more refined, plastic incarnation of Wicklund's "improved type of sled." His

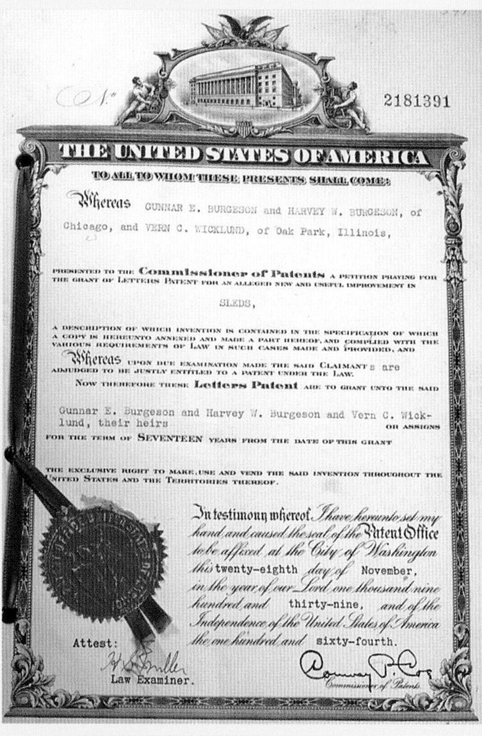
No 2181391

THE UNITED STATES OF AMERICA

TO ALL TO WHOM THESE PRESENTS SHALL COME:

Whereas GUNNAR E. BURGESON and HARVEY W. BURGESON, of Chicago, and VERN C. WICKLUND, of Oak Park, Illinois,

PRESENTED TO THE Commissioner of Patents A PETITION PRAYING FOR THE GRANT OF LETTERS PATENT FOR AN ALLEGED NEW AND USEFUL IMPROVEMENT IN

SLEDS,

A DESCRIPTION OF WHICH INVENTION IS CONTAINED IN THE SPECIFICATION OF WHICH A COPY IS HEREUNTO ANNEXED AND MADE A PART HEREOF, AND COMPLIED WITH THE VARIOUS REQUIREMENTS OF LAW IN SUCH CASES MADE AND PROVIDED, AND

Whereas UPON DUE EXAMINATION MADE THE SAID CLAIMANTs are ADJUDGED TO BE JUSTLY ENTITLED TO A PATENT UNDER THE LAW.

NOW THEREFORE THESE Letters Patent ARE TO GRANT UNTO THE SAID Gunnar E. Burgeson and Harvey W. Burgeson and Vern C. Wicklund, their heirs OR ASSIGNS FOR THE TERM OF SEVENTEEN YEARS FROM THE DATE OF THIS GRANT

THE EXCLUSIVE RIGHT TO MAKE, USE AND VEND THE SAID INVENTION THROUGHOUT THE UNITED STATES AND THE TERRITORIES THEREOF.

In testimony whereof I have hereunto set my hand and caused the seal of the Patent Office to be affixed at the City of Washington this twenty-eighth day of November, in the year of our Lord one thousand nine hundred and thirty-nine, and of the Independence of the United States of America the one hundred and sixty-fourth.

Attest:

Law Examiner.

Commissioner of Patents

invention, like Wicklund's, sprang from necessity. "My wife was pregnant," he recalls, "and told me I had to do something to get my two daughters out of the house or she was going to go crazy." It was Christmas morning, 1965, in snowy Muskegon, Michigan. The surf craze had swept the nation, penetrating even the snowbelt states, and by simply lashing two old skis together for his daughters, Poppen unwittingly shaped the lives of millions more kids to come. The Snurfer was patented and licensed to the toy company Brunswick Manufacturing, which went on to sell nearly a million boards through department stores over the next ten years. A handful of young customers included

// **OPPOSITE:** Wicklund's original patent. // **ABOVE:** Snowboarding, c. 1918 // **BELOW:** "It was like watching a Zapruder film," David Schriber wrote in a story for the premier issue of *The Snowboard Journal* where these photos first appeared. "Silent. Grainy. Recorded history." Wicklund's first linked snowboard turns, pictured here, were captured on film in 1939 at the Nordic Hills Country Club in Chicago.

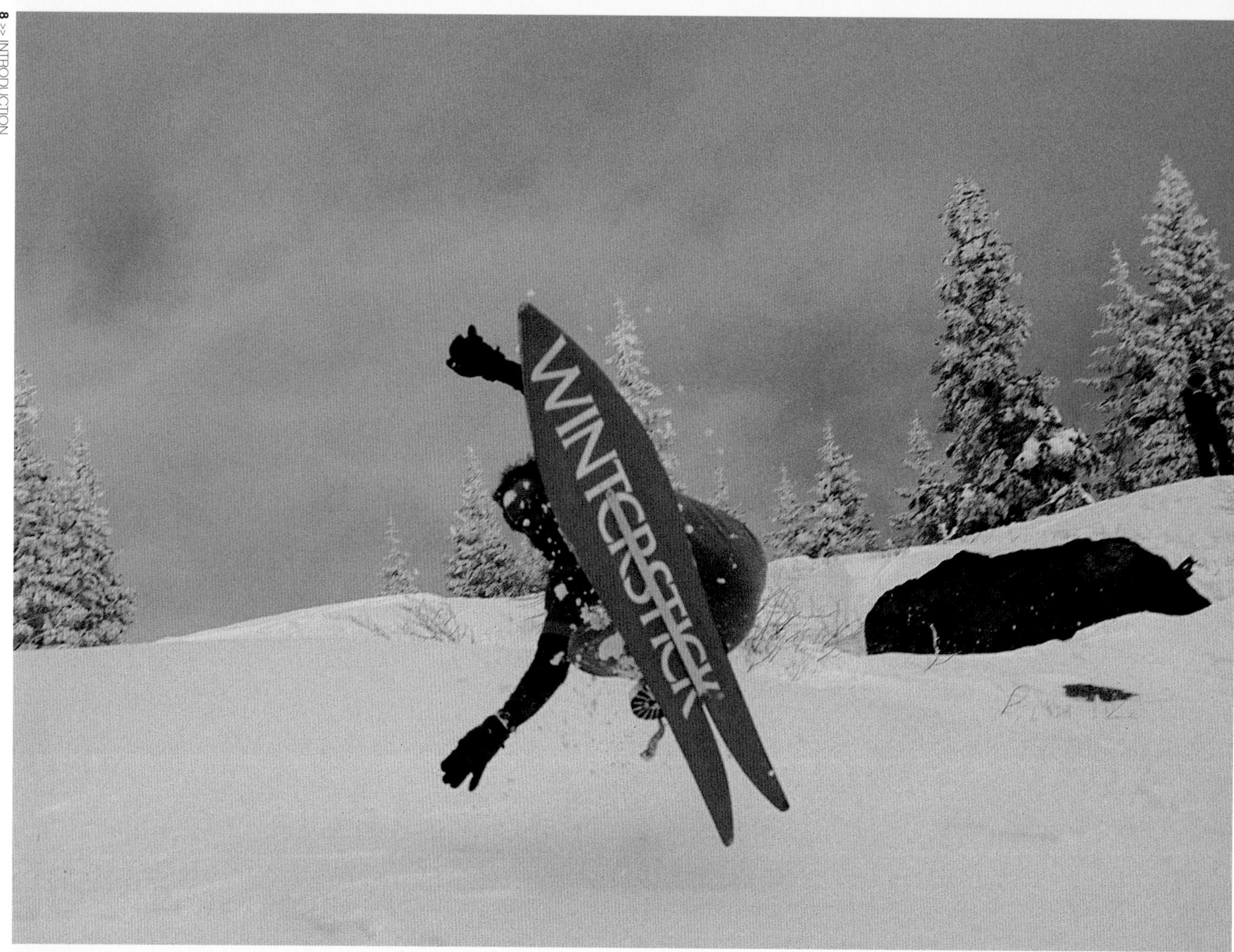

Jake Burton Carpenter, the Long Island native who'd go on to found Burton Snowboards in 1977; Chris Sanders, a Lake Tahoe local whose homemade boards eventually became Avalanche Snowboards in 1982; Mike Olson, the Seattle surfer who dropped out of college to start Gnu Snowboards in 1983; and Dimitrije Milovich, who moved from New York to Utah in 1972 to start manufacturing the next product in the evolution toward today's boards, the Winterstick.

Like the flash of a brilliant meteor, the early Wintersticks lit up the atmosphere of snow sliding and winter sports, making a brief yet significant impact. An engineer by trade, Milovich pioneered the swallowtail (v-shaped) design and was the first to implement metal edges, a crucial addition for most riders who were subject to conditions other than the deep powder in Utah's Wasatch Mountains where Milovich was based. Wintersticks were sold throughout the late '70s with distribution in eleven countries. They received national press in both *Newsweek* and *Playboy* magazines in 1975 in "trend" pieces that highlighted the new sport of "Wintersticking." But Milovich was an engineer at heart, and in 1980, he left his Winterstick venture behind to pursue other things. Nevertheless, he's recognized as a significant contributor to snowboarding as we know it.

These individuals, together with Tom Sims, who found his way to snowboarding directly through skateboarding, combined their independent experiences and ideas and collectively brought this sport into being. Today, little over twenty years hence, snowboarding is a global sensation. Like rap music or the Internet, the act of surfing mountains represents one of the defining cultural phenomena of our lifetime. **//**

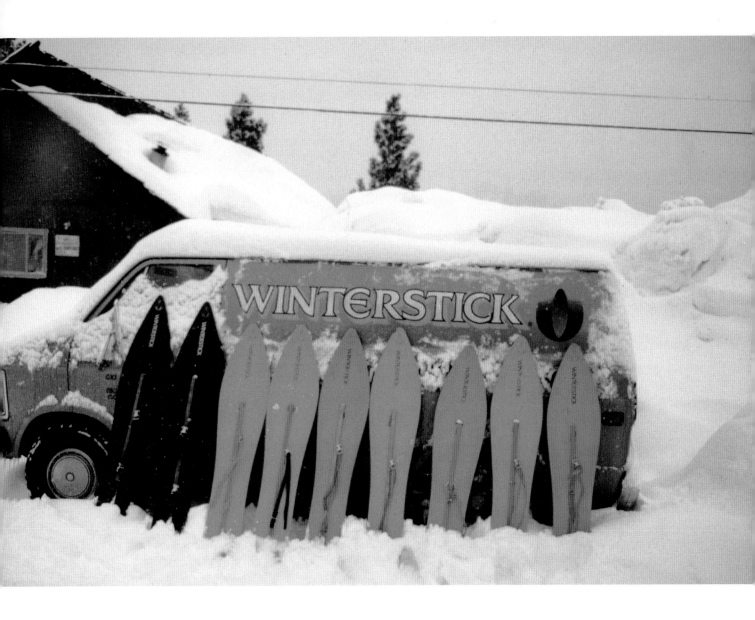

Natural and Easy to Learn

The Winterstick® provides you with an unrestricted choice of terrain. Previously unexplored areas like wind bowls, gullies and difficult back country, can be snow surfed, as can gently sloping open spaces (like golf courses) and many ski areas.

A loose snow surface with a 4 to 6 inch depth is all that's required. The Winterstick® performs equally well in soft, cold, knee-deep powder as in late afternoon, wet, cut-up spring slush; in fact any snow you can put your foot into. (The Winterstick® is not designed for use on ice, hardpack or unbreakable crust).

Because snow surfing's power comes from a natural turn-by-leaning movement, it is relatively easy to learn.

The Winterstick® is also extremely safe. There are no bindings to lock you to the board and the unique runaway leash / brake system keeps the Winterstick® from sailing down the hill without you.

The ankle leash attached to the keeper clip releases the brake during a fall.

Get Started!

Stabilize the Winterstick by digging the edge and tail into the snow.

Step onto the tail and slip your foot under the deck strap. This will anchor the board deeper into the snow, preventing a premature start.

Fasten the runaway leash to your ankle. Now step onto the front of the board and under the strap.

Clean the snow off your boots for better traction by twisting your foot against the deck texture. Reach back and tighten the deck strap snugly. Nudge the Winterstick forward. You're off!

The Winterstick® can be enjoyed without special equipment or clothing. Any lightweight and comfortable winter boots will work fine.

Once the basic snow surfing technique is mastered, the versatility of the Winterstick® can be realized. Soon, longer runs, new and exciting maneuvers, S-turns and jumps become possible. Often most exciting with a group of friends on an out-of-the-way hill, snow surfing becomes an adventure. The feeling is totally unique and exhilarating.

It happens with the Winterstick®

Begin Turning Stand over the Winterstick comfortably. Gradually lean to one side. Then press your toes down to tip the board further into the turn. Ahh! (shift your weight to your heels to turn the other way.)

Carve and Accelerate Sink down to the center of the board while tipping it into the turn to set the edge. Then extend dynamically through the carve. Whoosh!

Develop your technique...
Create your own Adventure

// **OPPOSITE:** Dimitrije Milovich is guaranteed a soft landing in the fluffiest of fluffy powder somewhere in the Utah back in 1982. // **ABOVE:** Milovich introducing his board line in an early incarnation of today's demo tour in 1980. // **LEFT:** This final catalog from 1980 is where Milovich left off before most had even started.

It's late December on Japan's northernmost island of Hokkaido. A foot of fresh snow blankets the local mountains and Jake Burton Carpenter is itching to make some turns. // The forty-nine-year-old CEO and founder of Burton Snowboards is here, in the resort town of Jozankei just outside the city of Sapporo, with his wife, Donna, and their three sons. The Carpenter family is halfway through a ten month world tour, which started back in July from their home in Stowe, Vermont. Having spent months travelling in the southern hemisphere, Jake is relieved and stoked that, once again, "winter is on." // Though it's getting late in the day, he's not one to let darkness stand between him and a powder session. The last few weeks found him in and around Tokyo, dividing his time between his family's action-packed itinerary, managing the company's Asian business affairs, and attending Burton's winter sales meeting in Colorado by video phone. Now he's starving not only for turns but to reconnect with Nature. He suits up and catches a ride to Nakayama Touge ski hill at the top of Nakayama Pass. It's already dusk and too late to buy a lift ticket. With a soft, vermilion alpenglow settling on the surrounding peaks, Jake grips his board under his arm and starts to hike. // Located on the southwest part of the island, adjacent to the Sea of Japan, this is Japan's powder capital. Home to 128 ski resorts, Hokkaido finds itself in a most favorable geologic location. Cold Siberian storms gather moisture as they rip across the sea, depositing six to ten inches of snow almost daily during the winter months. Many of the mountains in the region are perfectly conical volcanoes, rising from the sea to nearly 4,000 feet with plenty of above-treeline terrain. With the island's abundant natural hot springs (*rotemburo*)

// **OPPOSITE:** Jake Burton waiting on the tarmac in 2002.

/ OPPOSITE: Jake confirming that his boards ride fresh powder just fine. As he knows, one can never be too sure.

and a level of local hospitality and culture second to none in winter sports, there's little wonder why Hokkaido is a favorite among hardcore skiers and boarders such as Jake.

With factories and offices in both Europe and Japan, plus headquarters in Burlington, Vermont, Burton is the dominant global snowboarding brand. Despite fierce competition from hundreds of snowboarding upstarts, publicly funded snowboard companies, big ski brands, and other sporting-good giants, Burton has managed to maintain more market share—approximately one-third—than any other brand since the company was founded in 1977. Passionately involved with many aspects of the company, from its image to new-product development, Jake wears many hats. Today, it's a prototype Burton "Headphone Hat," which has speakers built into the ear flaps and an input for CD or MP3 players. His iPod is wailing Nirvana as he hikes into the twilight. At the summit, he can see in the distance the silhouette of a volcano. With a layer of clouds and fog lingering at its base, Yoteizan (Mount Fuji of Hokkaido) rises dramatically from the western horizon, lit from behind by the last breath of sunset.

With a foot of fresh snow, there's plenty of room for Jake to feel his way through each turn, carving silently around bamboo bushes without the benefit of total vision. The snow is light, like the fluffy powder in the western U.S. "This is what it's all about," Jake later writes as he describes the experience in the corresponence he maintained throughout this ten-month trip. It's the roots and soul of snowboarding, and it reminds him of back in the day when he would go to ski resorts at night when they were closed—because snowboarders weren't allowed on the mountain yet—to hike and take some runs with his friends. It's a reminder of how far the sport has come since he embraced it early on in 1977.

//

John Burton Carpenter was born in New York City on April 29, 1954. The youngest of four children, Jake, as he is known, grew up in Cedarhurst, New York, an upper-middle-class Long Island suburb. In the path of snowy Northeastern winter storms and in close proximity to both the city and the beach, Cedarhurst was a favorable if not ideal setting for a would-be snowboarding pioneer. At age seven, he was introduced to skiing at a small New York ski hill. Subsequent trips to Vermont with the family cinched his interest and planted the seed for what was to come.

Educated at top-notch New England boarding schools, the emphasis of Jake's upbringing was on pedigree. When he left for his first year at Brooks School, in North Andover, Massachusetts, at the age of fourteen, he didn't leave his Snurfer behind. While still a dedicated skier, he became hooked on the idea of surfing on the snow. A self-proclaimed underachiever, he was excused from Brooks for misbehavior after his first year, at which point he transferred to Connecticut's Marvelwood School. Conveniently enough, it was located at the base of a ski area. Despite skipping his junior year in order to ski and cope with the untimely passing of his mother, Jake managed to graduate from Marvelwood and enroll at the University of Colorado, Boulder.

However, all signs said that CU—and to some degree, skiing—needed serious rethinking. Inside of two weeks he broke his collarbone three times, once in a car accident en route to a Grateful Dead concert. The injuries dashed any hopes he had of NCAA skiing, and in a move influenced by his family's expectations, Jake ended up at New York University. Graduating in the spring of 1977 with a degree in economics and a subsequent career in finance, Jake foresaw a future he wanted no part of. "I was working crazy hours, and I had this feeling of futility," he remembers. "I felt a little lost." Inspired, however, by the entrepreneurial zeal inherent in Wall Street culture, he packed his bags, his Snurfers, and an $120,000 inheritance and moved to Londonderry—Vermont, that is. That same winter, Jake founded Burton Boards and started handcrafting wooden prototypes with a pin router in a barn.

His business experience limited to a high school landscaping outfit, this trial-by-fire operation burned through his inheritance and put the company $100,000 in the red. He'd overestimated sales, miscalculated the market, and ultimately put the horse before the cart. He realized he was selling boards for a sport that didn't exist, and that the future consequently was an open book. Burton pursued his vision for snowboarding's future, and worked with ski areas to set up competitions as a way to get snowboarders on to the hill.

By 1983, he'd held the first National Snowboarding Championships in Vermont and convinced Stratton Mountain, a major resort, to allow snowboarders. With a global picture in mind, he and his future wife, Donna, moved to Austria in 1985 and lived there for three years. Jake built a relationship with a factory where snowboards using the ski technology of P-tex bases and metal edges in lieu of skateboard construction could be manufactured, and Donna focused on distribution. Burton SportArtikel, the company's European headquarters, rooted operations in the Tyrol capital of Innsbruck and has since played a key role in how the sport matured throughout the continent.

//

Twenty years since Jake ventured to Austria in search of ski tech know-how and a European locale for his fledgling company, and more than halfway through his world tour, snowboarding's ultimate mogul is riding fresh powder at a small ski area just outside the town of Axams, Austria, site of the 1964 and 1976 Winter Olympics and not far from Innsbruck.

After Japan the Burton family landed in Europe where they spent an abundantly white and fluffy Christmas in the French Alps. "I rented a garage in the house next to ours and had the entire 2005 product line in there to test," Jake wrote. "I got to

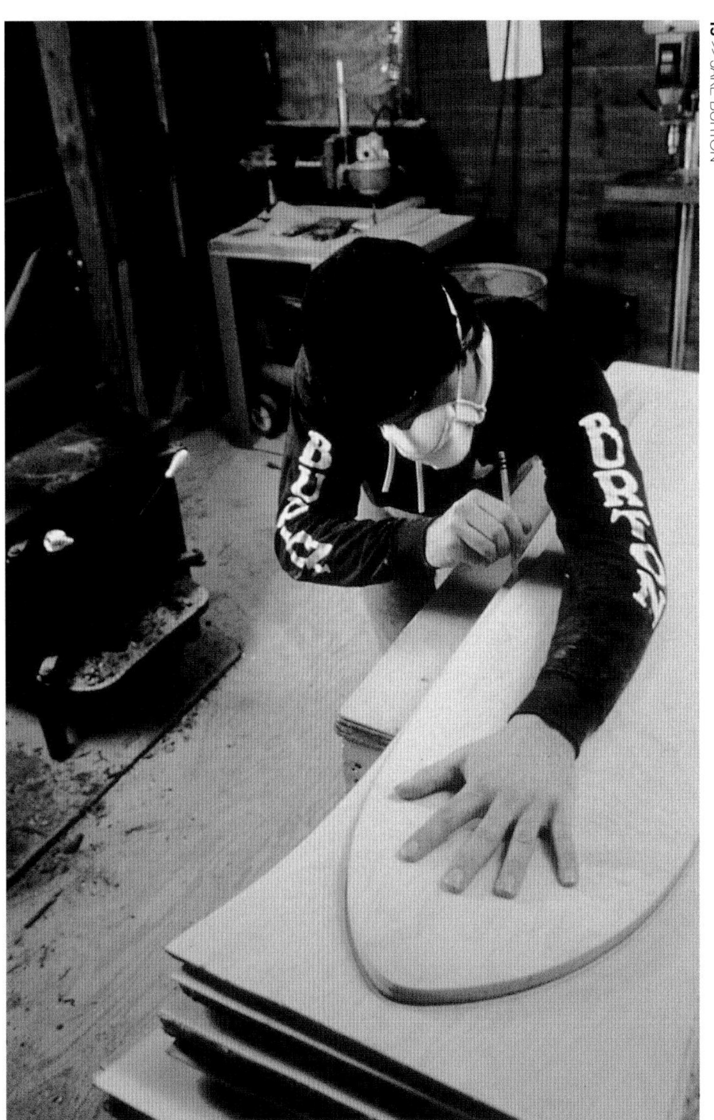

// **ABOVE, LEFT AND RIGHT:** Toiling away on a Burton Backhill in the company's first headquarters in a Londonderry, Vermont, barn c. 1980.

BURTON
SNOWBOARDS

// **CLOCKWISE FROM TOP LEFT:** Burton Backhill, 1982 // Burton Performer, 1985 // Burton Cruzer, 1986 // In 1990, after a short court battle with Vision and Sims, Burton debuted its first pro model, the Craig Kelly Air, with Kelly's now iconic signature // This Burton Safari from 1988 had a simple though classic graphic that captures the late '80s style.

// **OPPOSITE, TOP:** Though Burton's initial approach to snowboarding was racing, he was no stranger to taking air even in 1980. // **BOTTOM:** The Burton team in December of 1988. Back row from left: "D-Man", Jake Burton, Eric Webster, Steve Hayes, Mike Hayes; Front row from left: Andy Coghlan, Jack Coghlan, Scott Palmer, Jeff Brushie.

// Craig Kelly promotes himself and his new sponsor with this classic method-to-base-graphic-billboard air in 1989.

test damn near all of it." Jake's desire to ride every chance he gets and to put his personal stamp of approval on everything the company sells, right down to the Headphone Hat, is one way in which Burton stays ahead of so many competitors. And he hires people who share this same enthusiasm.

According to Burton's unwritten bylaws, fresh snow supercedes punctuality; almost by executive order, if it's a powder day, you ride first and come to work later. Invoking this ethos—one that arguably contributes to Burton's image as a core brand—Jake takes his time on the slopes of Axamer Lizum, enjoying its tree runs and kickers before he wraps up his business and heads to Italy for the Burton European Open.

Jake discovered early the value of promoting the sport ahead of the product in the days when he had a product but no sport. Lobbying for resort acceptance led to backing competitions such as the Nationals, which became the U.S. Open. Today, Burton sponsors three Open events, one each in North America, Europe, and Asia. The prestige of winning one of these events is immense, and snowboarding fans invest heavily in these champions. It took Jake until the late 1980s though to realize the power of the hero factor.

In 1987 Jake saw he was short on superstars and recruited World Champion Craig Kelly from his closest rival, Sims, to ride for Burton. Signing Craig and listening to what he had to say proved invaluable to the company, and consequently, to the sport. Since then, Jake has placed the utmost importance on sponsoring the sport's top riders and developing products with their input. In addition to Craig, Burton's first generation of stars included Shannon Dunn, Jeff Brushie, and Terje

Haakonsen. Today, it's Shaun White and Olympic gold medalists Kelly Clark and Ross Powers.

With Jake and his family in attendance, Powers claims the European Open halfpipe title, proving he's the best in the world—and that Burton's done well to back him.

//

It's now April. The family is in Switzerland, but Jake and one of his "Vermont bros" are surfing in Morocco. First they hit a spot he visited months ago near the town of Essaouira. "The waves were frickin' perfect," he says. "Head high to overhead and glassy, I was getting waves over a minute long." Then they move to a break known as Dracula's with "some very manageable double overhead surf." As the waves build throughout the session, though, the frequency of the set waves makes it tough to get out. In a fortunate lull, he squeezes through the exit zone and then reflects on the experience. "It's good to learn first hand that, like snowboarding in the backcountry, you always need to have a 'way out.'"

Drawing parallels between surfing and snowboarding comes easily to Jake. He has the utmost respect and admiration—you could even call it envy—for this sport of Hawaiian kings. It inspired him at a young age but eluded him well into adulthood.

"Since I lived near the ocean, surfing was always something that appealed to me," he recalls, "but my parents would never get me a surfboard, and I didn't have the money to buy one myself. Maybe that's been part of my drive for board sports."

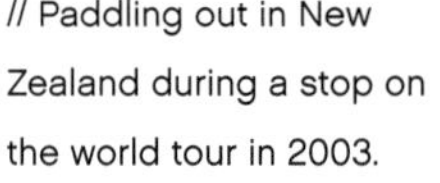

// Paddling out in New Zealand during a stop on the world tour in 2003.

// **OPPOSITE:** Riding some waist-deep New Zealand powder on Jake's endless winter excursion in 2003. // Burton slashes a powdery wave for lensman Jeff Curtes in the Southern Alps of New Zealand in the summer of 2002.

Though Jake gives skateboarding its due respect as an influence on snowboarding, he's more apt to praise surfing. "I think surfing deserves a lot of credit because surfing is the parent of all board sports. It's so cool because surfing is the most elusive and esoteric of the bunch in many ways."

Living in land-locked Stowe, Vermont, with a global company to run, Jake surfs only when he travels. For the world tour, this means every chance he gets. The Burton clan hit no fewer than twenty world-class breaks, at least one on each of the six continents. During a five hour layover in Lima, Peru, they squeezed in a quick city surf session and made it back to the plane, fed and showered, in time to fly to New Zealand. In Tonga, an island chain five hundred miles east of Fiji, they braved a small reef break in less than two feet of water. "I found it similar to backcountry snowboarding in avalanche conditions," he says. "The high is as much in surviving the session as it is in the ride itself."

Jake's trip culminates in Norway, the last stop on the family's endless winter. He's here to support and attend The Arctic Challenge, a premier contest organized by Terje Haakonsen, a long-time friend and Burton team rider. In the early hours of the day following the event, Terje takes him surfing in the frigid waters off the island of Stamsund. Walking through snow to get to the water and covered head to toe in a thick wetsuit, snowboarding's greatest businessman and it's greatest rider catch clean, head-high waves together. After lunch, Jake hikes the local mountain for a quick backcountry run.

"It was the last day of riding on the trip and the first day of my life that I surfed and snowboarded on the same day." **//**

As much as snowboarding owes its existence to the vision of certain individuals, it has emerged from a unique coalescence of earlier board sports. Snowboarding enjoys the benefit of reference points in surfing, skiing, and skateboarding from which to draw direction and inspiration. In a process that almost mirrors natural selection, snowboarding has appropriated the more powerful and favorable aspects of each, while establishing a heritage of its own.

Surfing, widely considered the grandfather of all action sports, dates back to ancient Polynesians who ventured east, discovering Hawaii and Hawaiian surf along with it. Surfing became a favorite pastime of Hawaiian royals and eventually its popularity spread throughout the islands and beyond. The sport traveled to Australia and the United States mainland, most notably Southern California, where a thriving beach subculture based largely around surfing established itself in the 1930s. The years of peace and prosperity that followed the end of World War II allowed the laid-back surfing lifestyle to flourish. "Somewhere between the Beat Generation and Hollywood, there was the beach, and the obscure sport of surfing was quietly thriving. The scene at Malibu was emblematic—a bohemian sideshow to the good life of the inland valleys and their concomitant American values" (Drew Kampion, *The Way of the Surfer*). This counterculture lifestyle that came to characterize surfing allowed room for the sport to develop according to the rules of the riders rather than mainstream mores. Snowboarding pioneers adopted a similar position outside the existing framework of winter sports to foster the growth of their sport as they saw fit.

The sport of skiing, though not technically a board sport, has a history not unlike surfing's. The first evidence of skiing comes from Stone Age rock carvings discovered around the Arctic rim that depict ski-shod hunters in hot pursuit of game. The modern era starts in Telemark, Norway, in the mid-1800s, where technological advances led to specific techniques for turning on a snow-covered slope. Men like Norway's Sondre Norheim and Austria's Johann "Hannes" Schneider became national heroes—mythic figures—for their great skills, pioneering achievements, and the national pride it afforded their countrymen. Immigrants from Norway and Austria brought their know-how to the United States around

// **LEFT:** The Arbor Element: This 2005 board design is a modern nod to snowboarding's roots in surfing. It features a thin slice of Hawaiian Koa, the same type of wood used by ancient Polynesians in building the earliest surfboards. For the Element, it acts as both a graphic and structural layer. // **OPPOSITE:** An old-school poma tow in the cradle of skiing: Hemsedal, Norway.

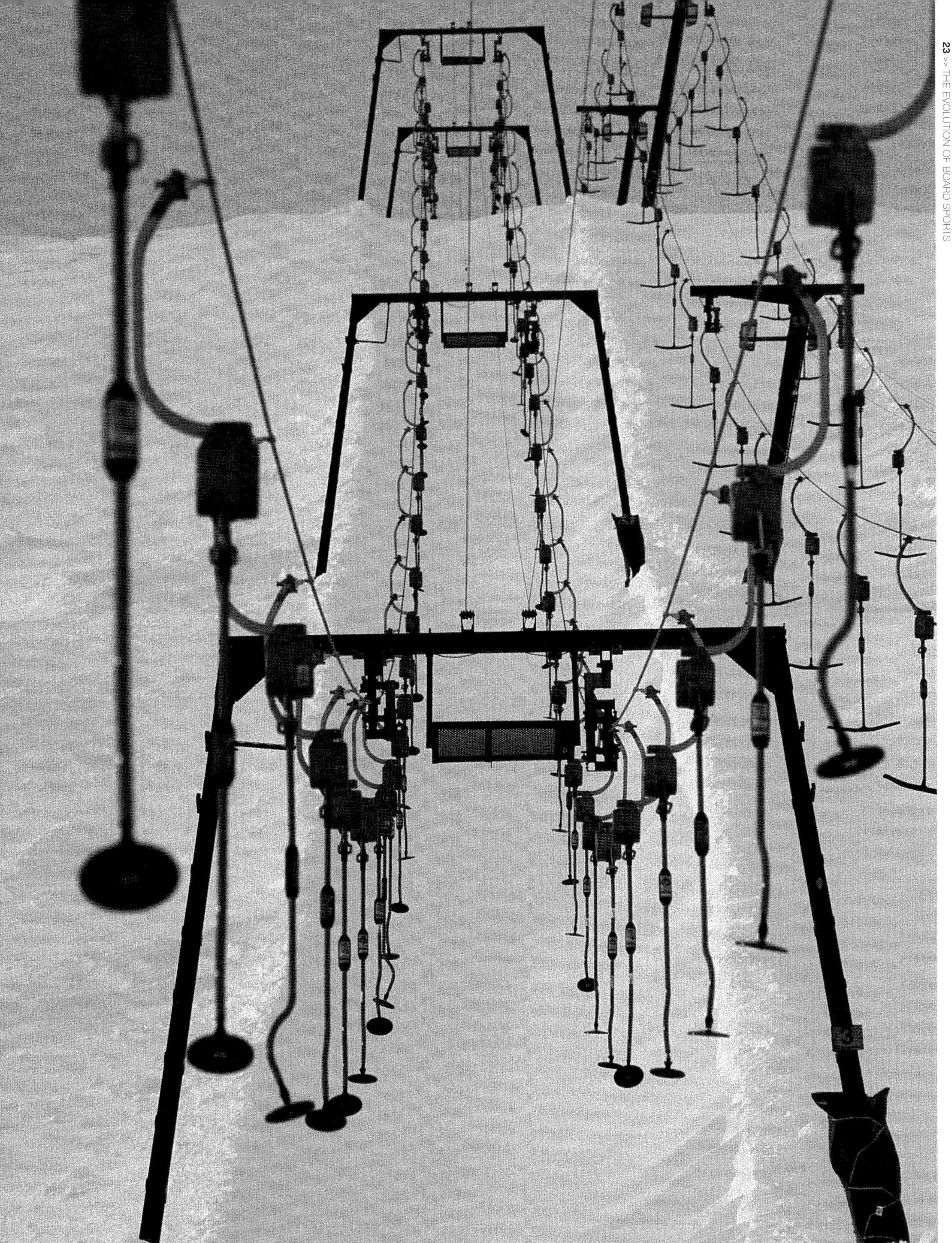

// **OPPOSITE:** Tom Sims high-sides it in a drainage ditch somewhere near Santa Barbara in 1975.

the turn of the nineteenth century, and skiing became modestly popular throughout the 1920s and '30s, mostly in the Northeast. One of the first ski instructors in the United States, a German named Otto Schniebs, taught skiing at Harvard and then Dartmouth in the '30s. His favorite sentiment, echoed around the East, was "Scheeing iss not a schport, it iss a vay of life."—a sentiment that would later find an echo in snowboarding devotees.

Rope-tow style ski lifts sprang up in the Northeast in the '30s, and, in 1935, the first overhead cable lift was built at Oak Hill in Hanover, New Hampshire. The skiing boom followed in the wake of World War II when returning servicemen, specifically those in the decorated 10th Mountain Division, pioneered outdoor sports such as skiing, climbing, and mountaineering. In all, some sixty-two resorts were either founded by, directed by, or had ski schools run by 10th Mountain veterans. Before the war, skiing was a diversion for a small, wealthy elite, but Americans' newfound affluence after the war's end made the sport accessible to a growing middle class. In 1955 there were sixty-eight resorts. Ten years later, that number shot up to 662. Small communities—ski towns—grew around many of these resorts, fostering the development of the burgeoning ski culture.

Skiing maintained a considerable mainstream contingent consisting of the racing circuit and upper class vacationers. In the 1970s skiing spawned its own rebellious offshoot, freestyle skiing. Moguls and inverted aerials gained popularity as a reaction to the strict rules of alpine racing, and while these skiers were hot-dogging in the mountains, surfers were taking to the streets, riding sidewalks and the urban landscape as an alternative to waves.

Though "sidewalk surfing" dates back to the late '50s, it wasn't until 1970 and the introduction of urethane wheels that skateboarding established a lasting presence. By 1975, slalom, downhill, and freestyle skateboarding were practiced by millions. Most notable at this time were the young surfers—the Z-Boys—who emerged from the Venice–Santa Monica area known as Dogtown, recently immortalized in Stacey Peralta's film *Dogtown and Z-Boys*.

The original Dogtown crew, including Tony Alva, Jay Adams, and Stacey Peralta, set the tone for skateboarding at the time and set the stage for skateboarding as a major cultural phenomenon. As young kids of ten to twelve years old, they lived in California's roughest surf community, many as outcasts. Their attitudes reflected it, and magazines captured it in living color. Coinciding with the punk rock movement, which was spreading from the U.K. to the U.S. at the same time, skateboarding conveyed a likeminded discontent: a backlash against conformity, the political establishment, and pop culture. For some, it was cool to be different. For others, who just didn't fit, skateboarding and punk rock offered acceptance.

Influenced by surfing techniques, specifically those of surf legend Larry Bertleman, skateboarders of the Dogtown crew dominated contests with an overtly surf style. They rode empty swimming pools, which served as concrete waves. Then, when riders started getting air over the lip, a new world of opportunity opened and vert skating took off. Concrete skate parks, such as the famed Del Mar Skate Ranch in Del Mar, California, popped up and groomed the best riders of the time—kids like Tony Hawk, who still dominates today. In 1980, however, skyrocketing insurance costs forced most parks to close and skateboarding entered a short recession.

It was during this time that one of skateboarding's pioneers and early champions, Tom Sims, shifted some of his attention to the snow. His Santa Barbara–based skateboard company was number one in the market. His wheels were legendary, and his team, which at one point included Lonnie Toft and Bert LaMar, had huge presence in the sport. Sims took his passions for skateboarding and surfing and headed for the mountains. **//**

It feels like tactical recon, peering through Tom Sims's military-grade binoculars. Only instead of scoping the enemy, we're checking out the surf several miles and about two thousand vertical feet below our position. We're on a hill at Sims's home in El Capitan Ranch, a secluded community of rustic estates north of Santa Barbara. The perch affords spectacular 360-degree views of the Santa Inez Mountains—their fertile arroyos to one side and a rare stretch of unspoiled California coastline to the other. Looking directly down on El Capitan Point, a famous and picturesque point break, we see a small cadre of surfers trading waves. The winter swell has been building all day; I know this not because I've witnessed it but because Sims—a board-sports pioneer, champion, and entrepreneur—has been watching and waiting. // "Yep, there he goes," he says, looking through the binoculars. "He got barreled." // Sims stands in an open doorway, which spills onto a porch and into his backyard. It's more like a grassy, manicured veranda than a yard, ending abruptly at a steep drop-off to scrub brush and who knows where. All you can see from Sims's den is this patch of grass, a ribbon of sky, and the Pacific Ocean smack-dab in the middle. He hands me the binoculars to see for myself—to share in his stoke—and starts thinking aloud, posing rhetorical questions, wondering whether he should grab a board and wetsuit and head down there to catch a barrel or two for himself. I half expect him to bail, leaving me here alone to pore through his boxes of old slides—boxes containing the full-color history of early West Coast snowboarding. Indeed, a random grab reveals a photo montage depicting not only the sport's most primitive moments but also the birth of freestyle.

// **OPPOSITE:** No pain, no gain—Tom Sims on a family trip to Mammoth Mountain, California, in 1999.

The surf does look good. Barrels are being had. Then again, a fog bank threatens to shut down the session altogether. Tom could get skunked. So, for the time being at least, we continue to sift through photos and chat about his legacy—one defined by so many innovations and vicissitudes.

Now in his mid-fifties, the board-sports champ has filled out around the edges. It's not that he's out of shape, but he's living well. He's comfortable. His once stringy blonde hair has turned brownish. It's thinning and receding only slightly, and he still wears a mustache. Though it's grayed with age, a soul patch on his chin reflects the hip and youthful exuberance that led him to board sports in the first place. "In the summer of '60, I saw some kids skateboarding in front of my grandmother's house in L.A.," he says, recalling one of many childhood visits to the west coast. "I was immediately enthralled and went into a trance, like, 'I wanna do that.'" In his eyes, especially when speaking about surfing or skating or snowboarding, you get a feel for the man's passion.

As any of the early pioneers will tell you, the good ol' days of snowboarding were not, in fact, so good. The technology, the market, the funding: it all seemed just out of reach. Trial and error leaned more toward the latter. New and aspiring competitors bogged down the bandwagon. An occasionally friendly but more often bitter rivalry brewed between Tom Sims and Jake Burton. They went head to head in every aspect of the new sport, vying for market share and the technological edge—both literally and figuratively. They competed on race courses. Each founded a major contest, one in the East and one in the West, which led to factory teams and the struggle for top riders. "The early '80s was a time of incredible product development," he says, "most of it driven by the desire of either the Burton team or my team to win the next competition." Tom Sims and Jake Burton saw eye to eye on just about nothing, save for the virtue and potential of snowboarding. "I remember being asked countless times in the late '80s, you know, 'Why is snowboarding growing faster than skiing?'" he says. "And my answer every time was, 'It's inherently more fun.'" On this, they could agree.

Sims follows his heart into everything he does. From an early age, he developed an insatiable urge to surf—to, in the broadest sense of the term, stand sideways with one foot behind the other and ride, whether it be on concrete, water, or snow. Timed such that it was, he came of age alongside the board-sports revolution. Destiny for Sims starts and ends with the board.

//

"It did snow in South Jersey," he asserts, "even if it was only two or five inches. And it didn't take me long to say to myself, 'I gotta make a skateboard for the snow.'"

Sims grew up in Haddonfield, New Jersey, during the 1950s and '60s. Having discovered skateboarding on a summer trip to California, he imported the

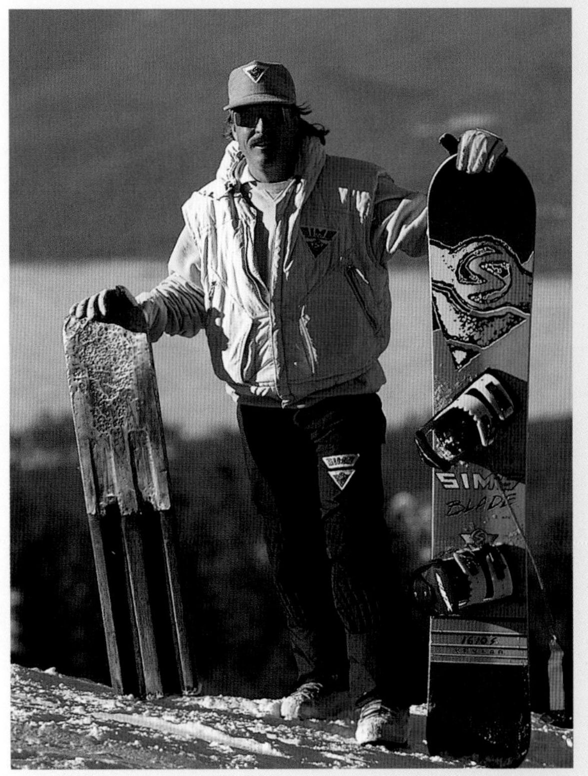

// Sims poses with his fabled seventh-grade woodshop "ski board" in one hand and his more contemporary Switchblade in 1988.

trend, which hadn't quite made its way to the East Coast at that time, and introduced skateboarding to a number of neighborhood friends. "We skateboarded every free moment," he remembers. "You know, before church and after church, before school and after school." When the store-bought versions failed—and they all failed—Sims built his own boards with old gear he would buy from a local roller skating place. He'd cut the skates with a hacksaw and bolt the two halves to a board.

Coincidentally, Sims was introduced to skiing in New Jersey the same year he happened upon skateboarding, the 1960–61 season. But there was no skiing in the neighborhood, "and when it snowed, I couldn't skateboard," he says. Applying the same brand of resourcefulness he'd used for skateboards, Sims took matters into his own hands. At age thirteen, fate offered him the unique opportunity to build something—anything—in seventh-grade woodshop.

"Well, I had built a boat, you know, a little model boat," he says. "And for that, I glued pine wood in layers and then planed the front. We couldn't use power tools, so I had to use a hand plane to put a kick on the front of the boat. Well, that clicked in my mind on how to put some kick on the front of a skateboard in order to ride down our snow-covered lawn in front of our house. Eventually, I put metal on the bottom and put U-nails on top and eventually added little bicycle inner tube straps to keep my feet from sliding off, 'cause it would ice up pretty quick. And the thing worked, and I rode."

This was 1963, and Sims is quick to point out that it was several years before Sherman Poppen introduced the Snurfer, the invention to which many other snowboard pioneers, including Jake Burton, attribute their first snowboarding experience. Furthermore, Sims draws a distinction between Snurfing and snowboarding: "For me, if a snowboard has a rope on the front, by definition it's Snurfing," he contends. "As soon as you take the rope off, you're snowboarding. That's my take on it—just like riding a scooter with the handle on the front. I'm talking about scooters of the '40s and '50s—once you break the handle off, you have a skateboard."

This line of reasoning, though sound, might also come off as self-serving. Not only does it marginalize

// **OPPOSITE:** The message to skiers was clear in this 1981 Sims ad: snowboarders get all the babes.

Burton's first boards, which featured hand ropes, but it seems to undercut Wicklund's early contribution to snowboarding. Poppen might argue that his version didn't require Wicklund's stick and was, therefore, different. This begs the question: Is a rope tied to the nose of a snowboard the same as a handle fixed to the nose of a skateboard?

Poppen, Milovich, and Burton found their muse in surfing, whether as participants or admirers, and their creations were envisioned either as pure recreation or as a backcountry alternative to skiing. Sims was the only early innovator to merge skateboarding with skiing. His somewhat controversial and now-infamous woodshop project, which is on display at the Vail Ski Museum, was for all intents and purposes, a skateboard for the snow. Sims called it a ski-board. "The fact that I was skiing and skateboarding, I just sort of combined the two," he says,"and I wanted to be able to take my board over to the local ski hill, Pine Hill in South Jersey. I was thinking, if I call it a ski-board, then they'll let me on the slopes. Didn't turn out that way."

In 1966, Sims rounded out his board-sports roots. "All of a sudden, surfing was a very big part of my life," he says, recalling trips to the Jersey shore as a teenager. "My dad bought me a gorgeous Miller Noserider for $155, and I was just in heaven." A couple years later, true to form, Sims started making his own surf boards. And then, in 1969, he came across surf legend Mike Doyle's invention for the snow: the Monoski. "I realized I had been making my snowboards too short," he says, "so I immediately took my surfboard building materials and I built my first full-sized snowboard, which was about 150 cm, and it was solid fiberglass, quarter-inch thick, kick in the front, no sidecut." After a few years at Hawthorne College in Southern New Hampshire, where Sims "basically snowboarded whenever there was snow," the lure of California's burgeoning surf-skate scene proved too enticing. Relocating to Santa Barbara "in '71 or '72," Sims built skateboards as a small business and sold paintings on the beach to get by. "But since I was such a surf Nazi and skateboarder," he recalls, "I didn't have much time for making income." That all changed with the onslaught of skateboarding's second boom.

//

Skateboarding flourished in various pockets along the California coast in the mid-1970s. The infamous Santa Monica–Venice Dogtown posse was one, and the Sims team in Santa Barbara was another. "Dogtown was urban surf-skate culture," Sims says. "They were into—I don't know what to call it—the whole 'bad boy' thing. What we had up in Santa Barbara was more of a soulful surf-skate culture. So you had these two different kinds of surf-skate cultures, and we were really the only two: the Dogtown guys and then the Sims team. It was all skateboarders riding the long skateboards, doing surf maneuvers."

In 1976, Tom Sims won the World Skateboard Championships based on the combined scores of freestyle and slalom, though he freely volunteers he wasn't the best. "At that time, I'd have to say Tony Alva and Jay Adams were both better skaters than I was." Well into his twenties at this point, Sims wasn't just a competitor. That same year he incorporated Sims Skateboards, "and by 1977 we were the number one skateboard company in the world," he says, "And during this time, I'm taking money that I'm making from skateboarding and putting it into snowboard research and design. I'm thinking that, at some point, others are gonna want to snowboard." In fact, Dimitrije Milovich was. He'd already received press in *Newsweek* and *Playboy* for his Utah-based Winterstick.

Chuck Barfoot, a fellow snowboarding pioneer, worked for Sims Skateboards at the time. After hours, he'd, "laminate up some fiberglass snowboards, because I'm allergic to fiberglass dust," Sims says. "So, while I'm trying to build a snowboard, trying to figure out a way to market it, Bob Webber contacts me, flies out to California, and says he has this tooling for a solid polyurethane deck. And he proposes that we put one of our wide Lonnie Toft skateboard decks on top." Toft rode for Sims as a pro skateboarder and had a signature model deck. By 1977, Webber had secured a patent for the "Ski-Board," one that more or less described how snowboards look and ride today. "As it turns out," Sims continues, "that's exactly what we did. Because we didn't have something we could market yet, we went ahead and did a partnership with Bob Webber. He didn't realize until he talked to me on the phone that I had been snowboarding since the early '60s, and that I had also been calling it ski-boarding."

According to Sims, this first commercially available Ski-Board, which Webber called the "Flying Yellow Banana," retailed for $79.95 in 1977. "We lost money on every board," Sims says, "but I was trying to get a sport off the ground." Of course, Sims wasn't alone, neither in the endeavor nor the frustrations.

The term "snowboarding" emerged around 1981 (although no one is certain of the exact year) as the general name for the sport; however, some still referred to it as "snow surfing." In the spring of 1981, snowboarders and Snurfers from both coasts converged on Ski Cooper, a small Summit County, Colorado, ski area, for the first ever snowboarding competition. Previous Snurfing competitions were mostly an East Coast phenomenon. The contest, consisting of slalom, aerials, and freestyle events, was called "King of the Mountain." Both Sims and Burton competed, putting their skills, equipment, and reputations on the line.

"I had built a special board for this competition, which was another solid fiberglass board, and I had sharpened the fiberglass so that there was a hard edge," Sims remembers. At this time, most other snowboards, including the Burtons and Wintersticks, employed surf-like fins. They were okay in fresh powder but had trouble turning on packed snow.

// **OPPOSITE, TOP:** The cover line of the 1981 *Action Now* magazine where this photo of Sims first appeared read, "Snowboarding: Is this the year?" // **OPPOSITE, BOTTOM:** The very first test mission of the board some called the Flying Yellow Banana, which fused a Sims skateboard deck with Bob Webber's Skiboard design, somewhere in California, c. 1979.

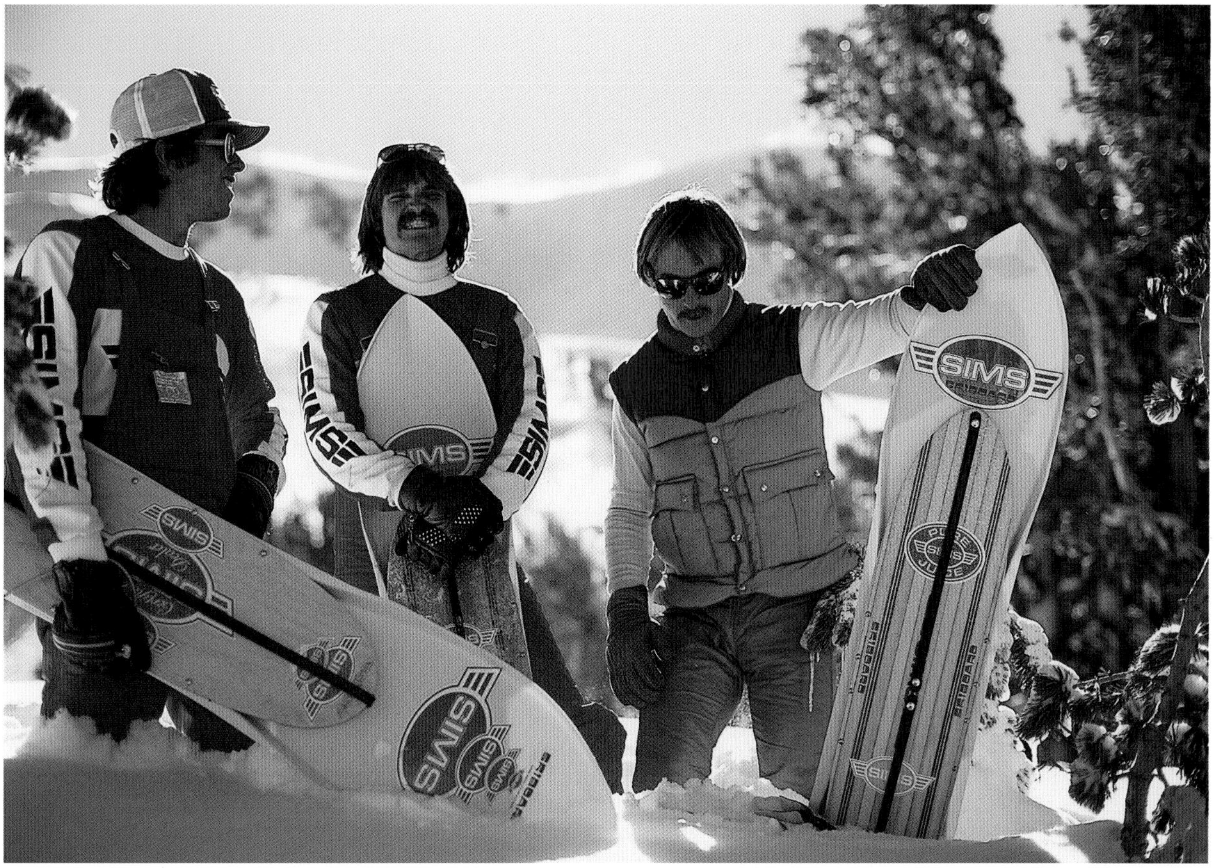

// Sims on course at the Slide Mountain Series in California, 1985.

"I was warming up on the NASTAR race course," Sims says, "assuming that's where they were going to have the competition. My board had a radical side-cut and sharp edges, and it was packed conditions."

The way Sims remembers it, "Burton saw me riding on the NASTAR course and realized that his boards weren't going to have a prayer. Demetrije [Milovich] realized his boards weren't going to have a prayer. So they pressured the contest organizer *not* to put the slalom on the NASTAR course but to put it down on the kiddy run, where no turns would be required." This was how Snurfer competitions had always been held, since they didn't turn well on packed snow. "So, right out of the shoot," Sims says, "I'm at loggerheads with Jake Burton." After all, Sims figured, "the reason they weren't allowing us on the slopes is because ski area management said we can't control the boards. I wanted to show them we could turn." Despite this disagreement, Sims won the slalom.

Tom Hsieh, a then-young San Francisco skate-boarder who later founded snowboarding's first magazine, *Absolutely Radical,* was there to experi-ence Sims's run first hand. "Tom had this technol-ogy that allowed him to perform on a level that guys on wooden boards with fins just couldn't. To watch a guy like Tom Sims come down the slalom course was just like, 'Wow, who is this guy?'"

The next year, Snurfing guru Paul Graves orga-nized the National Snowsurfing Championships at

ART CENTER
COLLEGE LIBRARY

// At the height of their rivalry, Jake Burton and Tom Sims put their differences aside long enough to pose for this photo at Purgatory Ski Resort in Colorado, 1988.

Vermont's Suicide Six ski area. One of the only West Coast entrants, Sims showed up with yet another board design. "I went down to the thrift store, the Salvation Army, and bought a pair of skis for five bucks," he says. "I unscrewed every metal edge, routed my snowboard, screwed on every little piece, filled it with epoxy, and sanded it down—so I had metal edges." Sims won the downhill, hitting speeds of fifty miles per hour, but broke his thumb at the finish. The slalom and overall went to Burton rider Doug Bouton. However, Sims explains, "I went down the slalom course as fast as I could go without falling, 'cause I didn't want to fall and have it look bad on TV." Indeed, the event was covered by *NBC Today* and *Good Morning America*, among others. "So [Doug Bouton] goes down, bombs the top part, crashes in a spectacular crash, gets back up, bombs the last part, and wins by a quarter of a second." This didn't jive with Sims's vision for the sport—nor did he particularly like losing. "I was quite frustrated because if you bombed it out of control, you had no chance of making a turn, so you had to fall, get back up, and then you could win. I was feeling embarrassed for the sport. That was another reason I felt I had to do the World Snowboard Championships in Lake Tahoe, where we'd have some nice turns, we wouldn't be going straight down the hill, and we'd have a halfpipe." Turning frustration into inspiration, he combined his skateboarding roots with the 1979 discovery by

// Sims launches out of the legendary Tahoe City halfpipe in 1983, the same year he introduced the first competitive halfpipe event and the first-ever ski area halfpipe at the World Snowboarding Championships in nearby Soda Springs, California.

Mark Anolik of the Tahoe City halfpipe, a natural gully located behind the Tahoe City Dump that Sims and his team had been riding for years. Taken together, he founded the Worlds in 1983 and forever changed snowboarding's competitive landscape—not to mention the physical terrain of most ski resorts today.

Again, the Sims and Burton contingents faced off. "When the Burton team came to Soda Springs in the spring of 1983," he says, "Burton took one look at the Sims riders coming down the halfpipe and formed a boycott." According to a story in *Transworld Snowboarding* magazine, "Burton team members threatened to boycott the event because they felt halfpipe had nothing to do with snowboarding and should not be considered in the overall." To be fair, though, introducing the half-pipe was akin to stacking the deck. Sims was setting an historic precedent, but it was in favor of his team. East Coast riders rode gates not halfpipes. In compromising with Burton, "I had to make the downhill dead straight," Sims says. "So again, on national television, here we go, straight down the hill, crashing, and that's what goes on the news."

Tom Hsieh remembers, "Ken Achenbach was accusing Tom Sims of improperly setting the gates for the slalom course." This stemmed from the fact that Sims would ride down the slope and have his team place gates where he made his turns. "It probably wasn't the fairest way to do it," Hsieh says, "but given that no one else was organizing races, it wasn't so far out of the ordinary. Tom was one of the more proficient riders at the time, and he was very competitive, even at his age, amongst all of the snowboarders. He had the best technology and his skateboard competitive nature was sort of crossing over into snowboarding."

//

From technology and athletic style to attitude and marketing savvy, Sims applied what he had learned from skateboarding to the emerging sport of snowboarding. He knew from experience that now that he had the boards, he needed to recruit the talent. Terry Kidwell was the first in Sims's arsenal of some of the best snowboarders around.

"I told Terry Kidwell, if he can win the World Snowboarding Championships, I would make him his own freestyle model," Sims remembers. "He immediately went out and won the Worlds. We sat down, and, on a piece of cardboard, designed the world's first freestyle board." In 1985, Kidwell's model featured the first rounded tail, as opposed to being split or squared off, and was the first to bear a pro's signature endorsement.

At this point, most boards featured P-tex bases and metal edges. Steadily, ski areas were welcoming snowboarders onto their slopes, and *Absolutely Radical* was renamed *International Snowboard*. The competitive stakes, once limited to trophies and bragging rights, swelled to include market share and brand identity. In hindsight, Sims's positioning was ideal; clearly, he was ahead of the

// **OPPOSITE:** Sims does a surf-inspired "layback-lookback" in the halfpipe at the 1985 Worlds in Soda Springs, California.

// **OPPOSITE:** A young Rob Morrow making a name for himself on the Sims team, Breckenridge, Colorado, c. 1986.

curve. For lack of funding, though, he had no choice but to seek partners. "I met with [ski manufacturers] K2 and Rossignol," Sims says. "I tried to convince them of the sport, but they and other people I approached to build snowboards or snowboard boots all felt that snowboarding was a fad, and by the time they got anything developed, the fad would be long gone." This led to a licensing deal with Vision, "who had been a Sims Skateboard distributor for years."

Sims's roster of top names—Kidwell, Rob Morrow, and Shaun Palmer to name a few—also included young Craig Kelly, who he'd discovered years ago at Mount Baker. Kelly won the Worlds in 1987, prompting Burton to (quite astutely) recruit the rising star away from the Sims team. This was the first blow in a series of setbacks for Sims. In 1990, Vision succumbed to financial troubles and bankruptcy, forcing Sims to sue for the rights to his name, losing momentum in the process. Throughout the '90s and to this day, the Sims Snowboarding brand has struggled to maintain its position in the market—the same one that Sims helped to build. "It's been frustrating for me not to be able to hook up with partners who had either the passion or vision or financial resources necessary to be real successful in this sport," he admits. "It's ironic, I guess, that so many of the early pioneers of the sport have gone by the wayside almost solely due to lack of funding at a very critical time in their histories." But, as they say, history is written by the winners.

In many ways, Sims traveled the most direct and pure route from surfing and skateboarding to snowboarding. Snurfing barely entered the picture for him. "The way I've always wanted to ride," he says, "is basically old-school Sunset Beach surfing, which is to turn as hard as you can."

Our interview winds down with a stroll around his property. There's a trampoline on the lawn. Under a covered patio, sharing a wall with his office, sits a halfpipe-style trick ramp for skateboarding. As if it were a family game room, skateboards and helmets hang in a rack like pool cues, inviting anyone to take a shot. Across the driveway, we enter the barn, a massive storage shed for his toys. Though many of his boards reside in museums, the barn alone tells a thorough history of skateboarding and snowboarding—not to mention his quiver of surfboards that could rival a shop. "I would say that, from day one 'til now," he mentions, somewhat reflectively, "riding with my friends and family is the most fun thing I can do." **//**

Long before snowboarders could showcase their skills in competitions or in front of the camera, snowboarding existed, without pretense or aspirations, in the backcountry. With deep powder, long hikes, and the absence of an established structure, this approach to riding—snowboarding's counterpart to soul surfing—would come to be known as freeriding. In the beginning, however, this definition didn't exist, nor was it necessary. It only came into being with the advent of freestyle, and to a lesser degree alpine racing, as a way to distinguish the type of snowboarding you did, and initially, the school of thought to which you subscribed. For some, freedom of expression in these nascent stages of snowboarding was best exercised by picking lines on the face of a distant peak; for others, it meant taking air and attempting tricks. The dynamic movements of vert skateboarding met the snow and freestyle was born.

One of the first venues for freestyle experimentation was a natural halfpipe discovered behind the local dump in Tahoe City, California. Attracting the interest of local riders, such as the Sims crew, snowboarders began launching, grabbing, tweaking, and landing like skateboarders on a ramp. They hiked up the hill to hit it again and again, eventually to the delight of photographers. They were showing off and forging new ground. One of them was Terry Kidwell.

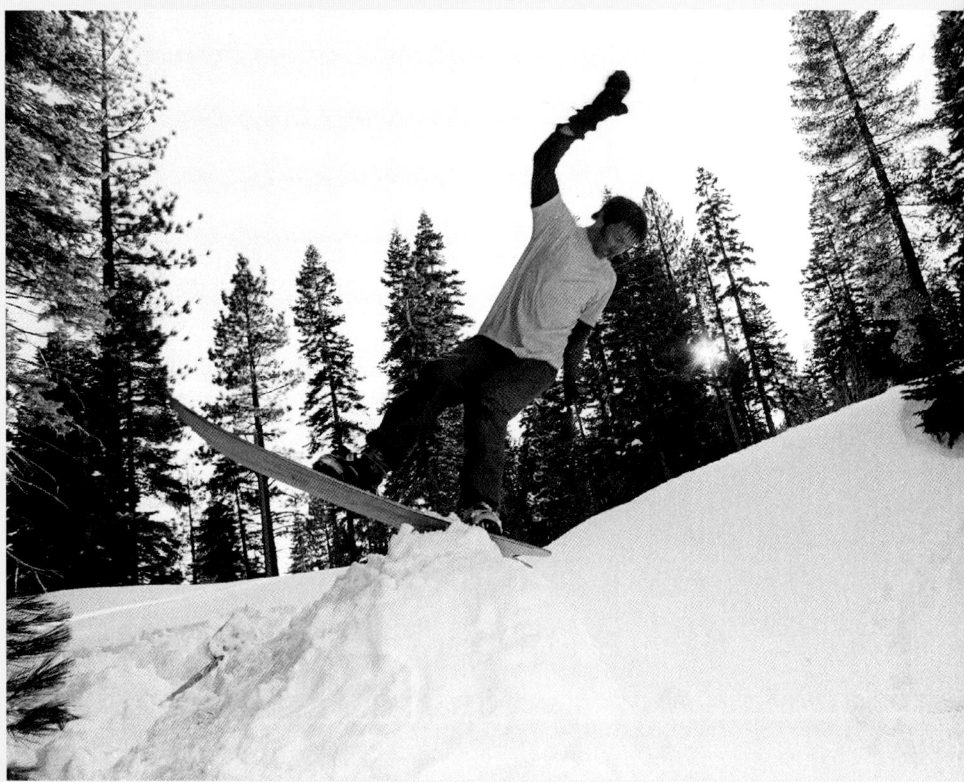

// **ABOVE:** Kidwell experimenting with lip tricks in a 1985 session at the Tahoe City halfpipe.

Dubbed "the father of freestyle" by many, Kidwell was an introverted kid from Tahoe who took to snowboarding like a bird to flight. Though he wasn't a freestyle skateboarder, Kidwell borrowed liberally from their bag of tricks—method airs, hand plants, mute grabs, and 360 spins—while adding a distinct snowboarding touch. His innovative riding style inspired countless thousands to go big and get stylish, laying the groundwork for what would eventually become an Olympic event.

As freestyle took root, alpine snowboarding (downhill and slalom racing) emerged as the primary competitive discipline, especially in the Northeast. Ski race culture set the tone, as the region was virtually insulated from the distractions of powder and the surf-skate scene when the halfpipe was introduced to competitive snowboarding in 1983, and freestyle became a judged sport. At this point riders didn't specialize in any one area—they shot for the overall title, though this wouldn't last long.

In the early 1990s, halfpipe snowboarding attracted tremendous national and international exposure, introducing the general public

// **ABOVE, LEFT:** The handplant, a direct import from skateboarding, at the Tahoe Donner quarterpipe in 1985. // **ABOVE, RIGHT:** In 1986, every young snowboarder wanted to do Terry Kidwell rocket grabs. Unfortunately, few had access to the Donner Quarterpipe, located between Sugar Bowl and Donner Ski Ranch. "No one rode it better than T.K.," says photographer Bud Fawcett.

// **FOLLOWING SPREAD:** Exaggerated mute grabs with a tweaked knee were emblematic of Brushie's unique style. // Damian Sanders promoting himself and his sponsor—older brother and Avalanche Snowboards founder Chris Sanders—in Nevada's Mount Rose back-country, 1988.

avalanche

// **TOP, BOTTOM RIGHT:** Damian Sanders in the role of snowboarding's original grom, at Slide Mountain in 1985 and at Boreal Ridge in 1988, respectively. // **BOTTOM, LEFT:** At the height of the neon craze in 1989, Sanders rocks hardshell boots, Vaurnet shades, Ocean Pacific clothing, and his signature headband at the first ever Squaw Valley contest.

to the sport through freestyle. It was showy and different, and several U.S. resorts built halfpipes for general use. With an abundance of attitude and sponsorship dollars, the next superstar was just around the corner, and, for the first time, he'd emerge not from California or Washington but from New England.

Born in Connecticut, Jeff Brushie found his way onto the initial Burton freestyle team, specializing in the halfpipe but also going big in all aspects of his riding. Brushie's style, from the way he rode to how he dressed and wore his hair, drew in young snowboarders by the thousands. Kids at the time wanted to be Brushie. He was the posterboy, the guy with the dreadlocks who sported Burton's latest duds and seemed to buck conventionality in all its forms. Brushie competed at the top of the game and helped usher the sport to new levels. He won the World Cup overall halfpipe title in 1991; the following year. Brushie underscored the growing rift between freestyle and alpine snowboarding by ripping a big method air while racing in the giant slalom at the June Mountain OP Pro contest in California. Bud Fawcett, on his way to the halfpipe, captured on film the sentiment of most snowboarders at the time: freestyle is where it's at. And it was.

Freestyle overflowed into the terrain of freeriding, and freestyle moves were integrated into overall riding on the rest of the mountain.

// **ABOVE:** The method air of snowboarding legend: Jeff Brushie on the GS course at the OP Pro, June Mountain, California.

Riders dropped cliffs and launched kickers with an ever-increasing bag of tricks. Damian Sanders will be remembered as one of the first to blur this line between freestyle and freeriding.

The brother of Chris Sanders, founder of Tahoe-based Avalanche Snowboards, Damian slashed his way into history as the sport's first rock star. Decked in dayglow with a headband and a big blonde Jeff Spicoli hairstyle, he went huge and fast for the camera. Sanders's skills, coupled with media savvy and his positive, upbeat persona, propelled him to the sport's zenith in the late 1980s. Starting out as a Southern California skater, Sanders imported a handful of tweaked-out board grabs, one known as his signature Iguana Air (grabbing the tail on the toeside edge), and then broke major ground by launching backflips and double backflips off cliffs. He graced the cover of *Snowboarder* magazine's premier issue in 1988, sporting green dayglow pants, and achieved instant superstardom with a role in *Snowboarders in Exile*, one of the sport's first documentary-style films. In one way or another, today's pros can attribute some part of their career and lifestyle to Sanders's efforts, even if they'd never be caught dead in dayglow. **//**

It feels like we're diffusing a bomb. I'm standing on a ledge, dissecting a five-foot wall of snow. This is a snowpit. In fact, it's shaped more like a wedge. Using shovels, we've quarried out a section of slope from a mountain of pristine powder here in the British Columbia backcountry. The floor measures five or six feet square, just room enough for the three of us: Craig Kelly, reclusive snowboarding icon; John "Buff" Buffery, legendary mountain guide; and me. The weather is socked in and it's snowing softly, almost eerily, with patches of light here and there. Craig and Buff get to work. // The vertical wall reveals a cross section of the season's snowpack, which averages forty-two feet in these parts, illuminating details about every centimeter of snow that's accumulated thus far, that is, through February 20, 2002. We've dug this pit to monitor and evaluate avalanche conditions. Through assessing the many layers and how they've bonded together (or not), Buff and Craig can better understand the snowpack's inner workings so they can make informed predictions about which slopes are stable and which ones aren't. Though it's far from an exact science, you wouldn't know it from their methods. Under magnifying glasses, they pick apart snow crystals like a jeweler checking the cut and clarity of a diamond. Craig measures the angle of the slope at a relatively steep forty-five degrees. Calculating snow temperatures at various depths, they each keep a notebook for logging the range of data. // The most dramatic and visceral part of the analysis, however, is the final step: the shear test. Buff first cuts a two-foot-wide column of snow out of the wall. Placing his shovel blade on top of the snow, he taps. When it doesn't move, he taps it some more and then hits it with his fist harder until finally

// **OPPOSITE:** Craig Kelly scopes terrain in the distance as the heli awaits.

it lets go. A small slab shears off, releasing into Buff's hand about a foot below the surface. Craig notes the depth and force it took to trigger this controlled, albeit minuscule, avalanche. I note to myself that the snow looks pretty stable. But what do I know? I'm really just here to ride with Craig Kelly.

Snowboarding's original soul rider is a partner in the Baldface venture, a snowcat skiing operation in Nelson, B.C. He lends his celebrity to promote the startup service, and helps out as a guide when available—that is, when he's not working his other job as team rider and visionary for Burton Snowboards. In 1987 Jake Burton recruited the up-and-coming star after Kelly won his first World Championship title. Kelly went on to overhaul and redefine the company's image, and he's represented Burton the world over ever since. In fact, Craig's just returned from a trip to Japan—from backcountry adventures in Hokkaido. Now he's ready to resume his training.

Studying under Buff's Jedilike tutelage, Craig is a young student in the art and science of mountain guiding. Certification by the Association of Canadian Mountain Guides (ACMG) is the consummate validation of your skills in all aspects of climbing, mountaineering, and avalanche safety. Buff, a backcountry guru, has been certified since 1989, and Craig seeks to become the ACMG's first fully-certified snowboarder. Though skiing is one of the ACMG disciplines—Buff skis when guiding clients—he opts for a snowboard today. After all, he's with Craig Kelly. . . .

Being out here, you get a sense that Buff knows mountain environments like a general knows the battlefield. And his reputation precedes him. While at a backcountry lodge near Whistler, fellow guides spoke of Buff with awe and respect, much in the same way fellow pro snowboarders speak of Craig. So there's an especially powerful dynamic here in the Selkirks: two legends of the mountain, each functioning as teacher and pupil alike.

As we finish up with the shear tests, Buff's radio crackles to life. The cat will meet us at the bottom for a lift. After covering the pit and strapping into our boards, Craig drops in first and, right below me, carves three flawless turns, one after the other, right down the forty-five-degree fall line. Witnessing this first hand, it seems clear from how he rides and how he performs in the backcountry that Craig was born for this—that he was born to guide not only clients but the sport as a whole.

//

The first-born son and one of the seven children of Pat Kelly and Janet Hansen, Craig Elmer Kelly entered the world on April Fool's Day, 1966. From an early age, Kelly cruised exceptionally through life's learning curve. He could already read when he got to kindergarten and then skipped the third grade altogether. But he was far from the skinny-geek-overachiever stereotype. Kelly possessed charisma, making friends easily through his engaging spirit and keen sense of humor. And, of course, there was his athletic ability. Whether

// **LEFT:** The boy king in 1987 after winning his first World Snowboarding Championship title for Team Sims. // **RIGHT:** 1990 World Snowboarding Championships in Breckenridge Colorado: Celebrating after a spectacular, (now legendary) halfpipe battle between Kelly and then-nemesis Shaun Palmer. It was almost too close to call, but the judges gave the championship to Palmer and Kelly conceded graciously.

playing football or picking up surfing, he could translate the intellectual into the physical, and let his body take over.

In 1979 the family moved to Mount Vernon, a town not far from Mount Baker Ski Area and the Canadian border. Thirteen-year-old Kelly was involved in competitive BMX racing at the time, and before long, he was sponsored by a local bike shop, Fulton's Schwinn. In 1981 the owner brought in a few Burton Backhill boards to demo and possibly rent out. Kelly tried one that winter near Mount Baker on a powdery slope off the side of a road and by the following year had one of his own. In the spring of 1982, Baker first allowed snowboarding on a trial basis, in part because mountain manager Duncan Howat was so impressed with Kelly's skills.

Kelly meanwhile was acing his way through high school, earning a 4.0 grade point average and on the fast track to higher education. His goal was medical school. During the winter of 1983, though, a different opportunity presented itself. The young talent was discovered by Tom Sims on his first trip to Mount Baker. "When I saw Craig ride," Sims remembers, "I knew he was special." Signing him with a free board—Sims's personal 1500 FE—and a handshake, Craig Kelly instantly became a sponsored Sims rider.

Still, the seventeen-year-old athlete and scholar maintained his focus and, staying true to the goals

// **LEFT:** Training tirelessly, methodically in the halfpipe, c. 1987. // **RIGHT:** Playing around near the Burton team house in Trukee, California, 1988.

he'd set, enrolled at the University of Washington to study chemical engineering. On the weekends, though, he rode. Or to put it more accurately, he practiced. Years later, Kelly revealed his methods in an interview with *International Snowboard* magazine. "When I train I'm very analytical," he said, "and I constantly think about working a certain muscle group or perfecting a particular technique. If my riding doesn't feel technically perfect, exactly the way it should, I concentrate completely on the problem. If I chatter out of a heel turn, I think, 'Why did that happen? Okay, next time put more weight on your heel foot.'"

While the sport of snowboarding searched for identity in the mid-1980s and struggled for resort acceptance, Kelly and his tight-knit crew—who'd banned together as the Mount Baker Hard Core (MBHC), the seminal snowboarding posse—progressed above and beyond what was considered "good" at the time. In 1985, eighteen-year-old Kelly took fourth in the inaugural Mount Baker Banked Slalom, trailing close behind Tom Sims, Terry Kidwell, and Ken Achenbach. Consistently placing top three in both slalom and halfpipe contests that year, he secured his first big win in the slalom event at the 1986 World Championships in Breckenridge, Colorado. A year later, Kelly was crowned World Champion at the very same event.

"He was going huge on the backside wall at the end of the pipe," recalls Tina Basich, who was there competing in her first Worlds. "And we had heard that that was Craig Kelly. His name was already a buzz in everybody's ear. And the next year, I saw an ad on the back cover of a magazine that had him hitting that jump."

The biggest move of Craig Kelly's career followed when he attempted to leave Sims, which was controlled and licensed by Vision at the time, and join the Burton team. As Jake Burton remembers, "It dawned on me that we were behind in regard to freestyle. It was clear that we needed riders, and Craig liked that we had our own factory and the ability to make anything he wanted." Vision/Sims and Burton went head-to-head in court, stemming from a contract Kelly signed when he was seventeen. By now, he'd made the decision to pursue snowboarding as a professional career, postponing college indefinitely with only fifteen credits left to graduate. The suit ruled in Burton's favor and gave birth to the signature "Craig Kelly Air," perhaps the most famous snowboard ever built. For teenagers at the time, it was *the* board to own.

Aboard his signature model, Kelly proceeded to win three more World Championship titles and three U.S. Open titles, along with the Baker Banked Slalom in 1988, '91, and '93. He etched for himself a new level of stature in the sport: the best snowboarder the world had ever known. His freestyle technique—the Kelly stance and his tweaked-out method airs, in particular—transcended that of the individual and quickly became *the way* to ride, the archetype for freestyle riding in general.

// **LEFT:** Kelly honing his edge control in 1985. // **OPPOSITE:** Blasting through (and over) the trees at Mount Baker in 1991, Kelly made the most of his career as one of the first fully sponsored freeriders.

By the end of the 1991 season, Kelly faced a crossroads. "I felt like I'd done everything I could with competition," he once told Jeff Galbraith, founding editor of *frequency* magazine. "I was just revolving at the same speed. I couldn't get any farther. I didn't feel like I was progressing personally in snowboarding."

"You'd have to talk to other great athletes, but after you've achieved everything you can achieve in a particular industry," posits Tom Hsieh, "you still have to get back to basics. And I think that's what Craig was searching for when he became more of a soul-surfing-type rider and adventurer and retired from the competitive scene."

Kelly left the party while he was still having fun—while he was still on top. He started the '91 season winning the Baker Banked Slalom and finished with a first at the Arapahoe Basin/Body Glove contest in Colorado. And sure enough, he left the freestyle scene to pursue something greater, a deeper calling of sorts, in the backcountry. Some might have thought it was career suicide, but his sponsors, who placed tremendous faith in the hero, backed Kelly one-hundred percent.

//

"Snowboarding is something that I think should be done on your own terms," Kelly told Japan's *SNOWing Magazine* in 1992. "Society is full of rules, and I use the time I spend in the mountains as an opportunity to free myself of all constraints. During the past winter I decided that competing on the World Tour restricted the freedom that I found with snowboarding in the first place, so I decided to try a year with very little competing. Now that I have

recap[illegible]e feeling that made snowboarding special to me, I am not about to give it up. This is not retirement. I am simply revolving my snowboarding professionalism around freeriding rather than competing. It sure feels right."

Throughout the 1990s, Kelly took snowboarding in a new direction and further honed his craft, setting a certain standard for freeriding. Performing for the cameras, as films became the new medium through which people experienced Kelly's riding, he didn't necessarily go the biggest or ride the steepest lines. No records were being set. With a sixth sense for picking interesting lines, he sought not "the most dangerous one but the one that feels the best—the grooviest," he told Galbraith, and you could see from every turn he made that he was groovin'. His signature style flowed with the terrain like equal forces at odds and in perfect harmony. Try as they might, few have been able to make it look that smooth.

Kelly continued his role as team rider and spokesman for Burton Snowboards. "The relationship between Craig Kelly and Burton had such an incredible amount to do with the progression of the sport," says Jake Burton, "and the progression and success of Burton as a brand." Although he didn't compete, Kelly still acted as a "media tool" for the company. "But more importantly," Kelly told *MountainZone.com* in 2000, "I'm a big research and development person. I like helping design products and dialing in what they have, so that's still a really active part of what I do." In recent years he helped

// **OPPOSITE:** The soul in this steep toe-side turn just about sums up Kelly's contribution to snowboarding. // **RIGHT:** This grab may be a stale fish, but the snow, the air, and the sunset are all fresh. Kelly rides the infamous "Mystery Air" with its blank base, per court orders, amidst the Sims/Vision vs. Burton lawsuit.

// **OPPOSITE:** Craig Kelly at Island Lake in 1992.

develop (somewhat selfishly) the company's split-board design, a board that splits into skis for ascending backcountry terrain and then clamps back together to be ridden as a snowboard. In general, though, "His fingerprint is on so many Burton products," says John "JG" Gerndt, the company's in-house product designer, "I don't know if I'll ever be able to pick out a Burton snowboard that didn't somehow evolve because of Craig's input."

Though not a religious person in the traditional sense, Kelly's journey into the backcountry transcended the physical and mental elements of riding, those aspects of the game he commands with precision, and revealed something less tangible but all the more meaningful. "When I go out into the backcountry," he told *MountainZone.com*, "I sort of feel this elation at being out there and the purity and the freedom that comes with the experience. It sort of lends itself to believing that there is another dimension to everything that we do. It doesn't have to have anything to do with God necessarily—for a lot of people it would—or have anything to do self-actualization. But there's a feeling you get from certain things you do in life that just kind of feels pure and independent of what's actually, physically going on. All of a sudden you have this feeling of clarity."

One can only speculate that he experienced this same sense of purpose when, on a trip to Nelson in 1999, he met a masseuse named Savina Findlay. Immediately smitten with one another, the free-spirited couple soon embarked on a fourteen-month surfing trip along the west coasts of North and South America, from Alaska to Chile. During this hiatus from snowboarding, Kelly and Findlay lived in a four-wheel-drive Sportmobile campervan. Before returning home to British Columbia, they'd conceived and given birth to a daughter, Olivia Maria.

//

On January 21, 2003, a wave of shock and disbelief passed through the snowboarding community when word of Craig's death in an avalanche spread. Kelly had been working with Selkirk Mountain Experience (SME), a backcountry ski-touring outfit based in Revelstoke, British Columbia, about one hundred miles north of his home in the town of Nelson. Owned and operated by Swiss Mountain Guide, Reudi Beglinger, the company advertises "superb mountain skiing on the vast, pristine glaciers and countless alpine peaks surrounding the Durrand Glacier." Clients are flown by helicopter to the Durrand Glacier Chalet from where they base daily guided ski tours. Kelly was there to help out in preparing to take his guide-certification exam.

On January 18, 2003, Kelly and a group of nineteen clients arrived at the chalet and spent the day reviewing avalanche safety and rescue techniques, standard procedure for any type of guided backcountry outing. The Canadian Avalanche Association (CAA) deemed the avalanche risk "Considerable," which ranks halfway up the scale,

// **OPPOSITE:** Kelly at home in a steep couloir, 1996.

urging increased caution in steeper terrain. A travel advisory for the region further highlighted "two deeply buried problem layers [in the snowpack]" and went on to say that "any avalanche triggered on the older weakness may propagate extensively into a large and dangerous avalanche event."

The group of twenty-one skiers set out from the chalet on January 20 at 8:00 AM. Divided into two groups according to strength and ability, Beglinger led the faster of the two. Craig was asked to join them but declined, preferring to be near the back where he could monitor and help the guests ahead of him. Ken Wylie, an SME employee and certified guide, led the second group with Craig. The plan was to gather at the summit and ultimately ski together.

The final push ascended a steep gully: La Traviata, the west couloir of Tumbledown Mountain, a large peak overlooking the Durrand region. On a slope measuring thirty-five degrees, the lead group criss-crossed the face reaching the top just as the second started its climb. Shortly before 11:00 AM, with eight out of twelve of the first group on top, Beglinger reportedly heard what was described as a "shotgun blast," followed seconds later by a loud "whump" and a huge settlement of snow. Beglinger and his group had triggered a Class 3 avalanche.

To be more precise, three slides were triggered. As the avalanche report indicated, conditions were ripe for a domino effect of sorts. The third and fatal avalanche released just below Beglinger at the top of La Traviata. Measuring 200 feet across at the crown, the slide fractured to a depth of nearly five feet and ran 380 yards from the top of the couloir to a depression in the terrain at the bottom. It buried eleven skiers completely and two partially. A frantic search ensued. Six were rescued, seven succumbed to asphyxiation. The body of Craig Kelly was the last to be recovered, buried under more than ten feet of snow. Due to the magnitude of the avalanche and the nature of the terrain and where Kelly was standing at the time, he didn't stand a chance.

Most agree Kelly knew and accepted the risks, that he lived life to the fullest doing what he loved to the very end, and that the backcountry is too unpredictable for one to always make the right decisions. These thoughts give comfort, no doubt, but they offer little explanation. It's easy to chock it up to fate or to shit happening, but the warning signs were there, and every precaution was *not* taken. No one dug a snowpit. If someone had, they may have discovered the "two deeply buried problem layers that need[ed] continued attention," just as the CAA bulletin warned. Perhaps the second group would have waited in a safe zone for the first to clear the couloir. Of course, this is clear only with twenty-twenty hindsight.

//

To the world of snowboarding, losing Craig Kelly was like the passing of a Pope or the untimely death of Princess Diana, resonating with immeasurable grief. News of the tragedy spread just as fast and left the same feeling of loss in its wake.

On the night of Craig's burial, a group of friends from Nelson, Buff included, fashioned a wooden cross out of two-by-fours and hiked it up the mountain. "Craig was with us," Buff remembers, "and we each talked to him in turn. I don't know why I plunged the cross near those rocks in mid-January, but there it lived in balance with the soft Kootenay snow and scouring winds for the remaining winter." At the European Open that year, organizers cancelled one day of the contest and replaced it with a day of freeriding in honor of the fallen hero.

"I can't think of a bigger loss to the sport and to all of us personally," said Jake Burton. "Craig was the epitome of core: to be the World Freestyle Champion four times and rule the sport the way he did was a huge accomplishment, but to retire from competing and go on to become a backcountry guide says far more about him."

"I met Craig in 1989," fellow Burton team member Terje Haakonsen recalls. "He was my inspiration. When I finally met him he turned out to be the best possible role model. He has always been the mentor for my friends and me. Not just because of his snowboarding but also for his lifestyle and love for the mountains. I don't know anybody else that loved mountain riding as much as he did. Nor do I know anybody who had the style and grace coming down the mountain. Having Craig leaving us, he will still be my greatest mentor."

"My eyes well up when I think about him," said Tom Sims, "how in tune he was with himself, how in tune he was with Nature. This guy was a Zen snowboarder, and it was a sacred experience for him, the backcountry. He sacrificed material wealth to seek oneness with his riding and the backcountry. The guy's awesome, and he lives forever." **//**

// OPPOSITE: "This is Craig standing amongst the cornices on Mushi Mushi ridge," says Baldface Lodge cofounder Paula Pensiero. It's meaningful because it is where a cross has stood since the night of his death. His friends and family have come to the cross with rocks from all over the world to honor his memory. We plan to have a huge raven carved to be a permanent memorial for him."

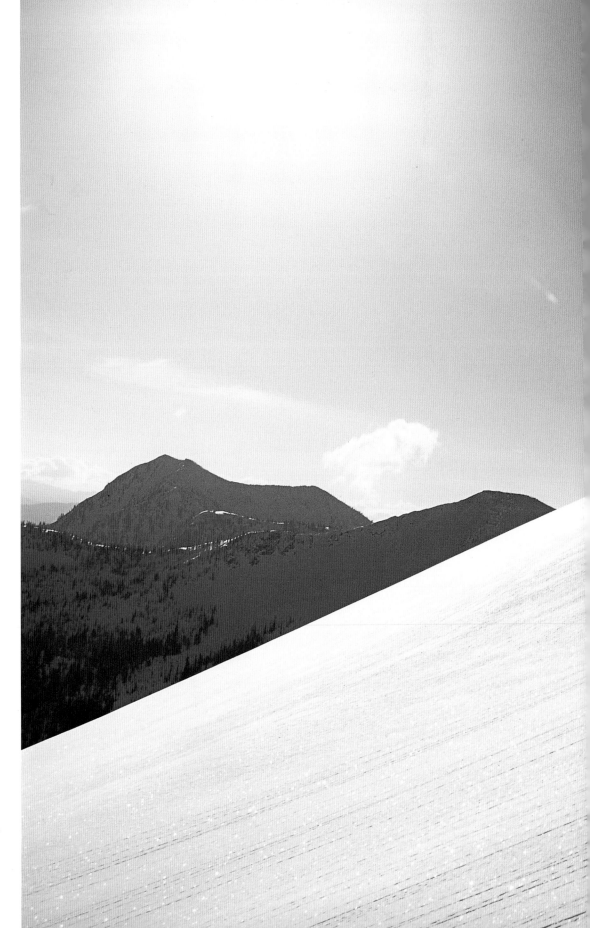

// Taken on a day of heli-skiing near Kelly's home in Nelson, B.C., this session in 2002 was the last time Burton photographer Jeff Curtes worked with Craig before his untimely death.

IN MEMORIAM: CRAIG KELLY, 1966–2003

The pilot circles around so that we—five snowboarder-clients and one skier-guide— can get a better look at the lines on Caffeine Ridge, a magnificent amphitheater of pristine powder in Alaska's Takhinsha Mountains. We're scoping for route options, for various ways down the forty-five-degree face, which drops three thousand vertical feet to the valley. When you're heli-boarding in the Frontier State, knowing your line is tantamount to surviving it. Alaska—the fabled North Shore of snowboarding—serves up some of the biggest and most celebrated terrain in the world. It's a place where mythic lines and narrow escapes give way to snowboarding legend. // With the exactitude and care of a surgeon, our pilot, Al, who once flew helicopters in Vietnam, sets her down ever-so-gently and waits for us to unload. Huddled in a pile, holding down our gear, our guide Cody signals the OK. With this, Al pulls back on the stick. The rotors reverberate against my body with a deep *thwump-thwump-thwump* as the bird lifts off and then banks over the cliff. The last thing we see is a contrail of snow streaming off its skids as the rotor wash settles. Then it's quiet. In the offing, where the terrain rolls away, a solitary figure stands with his back to us. Like a bird of prey, he surveys the scene unfolding below him. It's Tom Burt, lead guide for the heli-skiing outfit, Out of Bounds Adventures. He's watching riders from another group—pros working with a film crew—negotiate their lines. These riders hang it out in harm's way for a living, only here, they feel a bit more comfortable knowing Tom Burt is watching. // Burt is the sport's ambassador to severe terrain, the humble master of impossibly steep lines—in particular, those where a mistake can and will cost you your life. What sets him apart from

// **OPPOSITE:** Tom Burt surveying the landscape and his line in Alaska's fabled Chugach Mountains, 1997.

VUARNET
ICE AGE

other big-mountain riders, though, is technique. Burt rides "with a graceful style not typically associated with such extreme endeavors," wrote Rob Story in a 2001 profile. Having "defined the still-esoteric genre of snowboard mountaineering . . . Burt has chalked up more than forty first descents. Big ones: He and [longtime partner Jim] Zellers are the first humans to have surfed Peru's Cordillera Blanca, Nepal's Mount Pumori, Mexico's Mount Orizaba, and Alaska's Mount McKinley, among other 20,000-foot giants."

With twenty years of professional snowboarding under his belt, T.B. (as he's known) assumes the role of tribal elder, not as some sort of pretension but by the very fact that he's forty and still the best at what he does. In a sport where most are lucky to have three or four years in the spotlight, he's achieved a certain level of immortality. But you won't find this fourth-generation Tahoe native anywhere near a terrain park or halfpipe. Unless he's dropping a cliff that can't otherwise be avoided, he's not one to catch air for the sake of catching air. And if there's no fresh snow left, you're not likely to find him riding in-bounds at a ski resort. Whether in Tahoe or Alaska or some peak in the Himalayas, Burt's inspiration—his *raison détente*—is derived from the backcountry experience.

On Caffeine Ridge, in this magnificent yet unforgiving environment, the man seems perfectly at home. With his group safely to the bottom, he turns his attention to us. "There's about an inch of snow on top that could slide," he advises, "so be careful."

A constant wind blasts snow crystals up and over the slope as we peer over the edge, trying to recall what we saw from the air. T.B. hikes to the top of one of the spines to get a better view and (let's be honest) a more enticing line. Cody positions himself on an outcropping with a clear view to the bottom. Strapped in and with the green light to go, this is the most tense moment. You envision the first couple turns and pick out a safe zone—an escape route in the event of an avalanche. The rest will happen instinctually and from memory. Over the course of the last week, I've learned a thing or two about the mystique surrounding Alaska's snowboarding scene and that of its patron saint.

//

The Alaskan heli-skiing phenomenon started in Valdez and Juneau almost simultaneously, around 1990, when local skiers and snowboarders convinced local pilots to give them a lift. Since then, it's blossomed into a cottage industry where diehards make the long pilgrimage each spring, and a day of snowboarding can cost $1,000. In the early '90s, Tom Burt, along with cohorts Jim Zellers and Bonnie Leary, arranged heli trips with a Juneau local known to most in snowboarding's top echelon by first name only—or, rather, by an affable likeness of it. "Sean Dog" Brownell pioneered the business of heli-skiing here in Alaska's southwest region. Founded in 1992, his company, Out of Bounds Adventures (OBA), operated along Alaska's Inside Passage between Juneau and Skagway,

// Polaroid photos are used to study technical and potentially hazardous lines so riders can have the clearest possible idea of how they'll attack each section.

eventually deciding on Haines for a permanent base. Located at the crux of America's longest fjord, just an hour's flight or five-hour ferry from Juneau, this picturesque fishing hamlet of 2,500 year-round residents once marked the gateway to the Yukon gold rush. For snowboarders looking to mine fresh turns, it's just thirty-three miles from there to the helipad.

I'm right on schedule, traveling north on historic Haines Highway, curving along the banks of Chilkat River en route to the Canadian border. I was told by Sean Dog to meet him and Burt at "33 Mile" around 9:00 AM. Watching intently as the miles tick by on my rental car's tripometer, I'm not really sure what to expect when it gets to 33. In fact, 33 Mile is both the name *and* location (on the Haines Highway) of a certain roadhouse café—the one with the helicopter parked out front, and the last chance for a greasy breakfast before either crossing the border into Canada or boarding a chopper for the Promised Land. Unfortunately for me, paradise is socked in with clouds when I arrive and for the moment, we're grounded. It may clear, but any optimism among the guides seems more like wishful thinking. Welcome to the Alaskan down day.

Being so close to the water—Glacier Bay and the Gulf of Alaska are just the other side of these mountains—this area sees a fair share of clouds from the onshore flow. I'm told, however, that Haines is blessed with more blue-sky days than other parts of Alaska, so there's a good chance we'll fly tomorrow. In the meantime, we fish.

// **ABOVE:** An original member of the Tahoe-based Avalanche team, Burt's method airs are distinctive but not why he's considered one of the best riders ever. // **RIGHT:** At the Sierra Snowboard Championships in 1985.

Burt grabs a couple rods, and we drive the few miles back toward Haines to a spot on the Klehini River. A few of the guides and locals are already there, yanking small rainbow and Dolly Varden trout out of the murky brown runoff. Burt, the youngest of five children, grew up simply—poor, you could say—on the shores of Lake Tahoe, and he counts fishing as a day well spent. It's one step closer to living life by his personal ideals, by the set of principles he adopted some years back from Steinbeck's *About Ed Ricketts*: "Number one and first in importance, we must have as much fun as we can with what we have. Number two, we must eat as well as we can, because if we don't we won't have the health and strength to have as much fun as we might. And number three and third and last in importance, we must keep the house reasonably in order, wash the dishes, and such things. But we will not let the last interfere with the other two."

"I never really pursued [a snowboarding career] that hard," he says, casting a rusted, spoon-shaped lure into the river. "It wasn't my mission in life. I wasn't trying to make money in this sport."

If you don't know Tom Burt, this attitude might come off as sour grapes. But he had every opportunity to capitalize on his talent—to rake in the dough like Shaun Palmer or Rob Morrow—and opted instead to follow those three principles. Playing the game as it was being played just wasn't fun for Burt. Besides, he had bigger things in mind.

// Chilling at the '85 Worlds, from left: Tom Burt, Jim Zellers, an unidentified shredder, and Mark Heingartner.

"I started skiing when I was four and didn't start snowboarding until I was eighteen," he says. His family couldn't afford lift tickets, so Burt took to hiking the backcountry at an early age. "We grew up in the era of 'short skis suck' and swivel-hipping bump fags," he remembers. "By the time I was a kid, it was not the thing to do. It was about going fast—about GS'ing the moguls." Hence, the foundation for Burt's style and attitude. In 1983, while attending college at the University of Nevada in Reno, he discovered snowboarding. Earning dual degrees in mathematics and education, he went on to teach for a year at a public high school in Sparks, Nevada.

"In 1984–85, I started going to resorts and did races for fun. I did well and got asked to be sponsored by Avalanche Snowboards," he says. "I was like, 'What does that mean?' They said, 'We'll give you a snowboard.' And that sounded like a fair deal." Burt competed in all events, including the halfpipe, of the first Worlds in Soda Springs and first Nationals in Vermont, consistently placing in the top ten. In 1987, following the Worlds in Breckenridge, Colorado, he, along with Jim Zellers, Craig Kelly, and Bert LaMar, appeared in the now-infamous Juicy Fruit commercial. It paid $24,000 over the next two years, plenty enough for Burt to declare himself a professional snowboarder and otherwise fund his backcountry endeavors. He and Zellers were already growing tired of the competitive circuit. "We knew we weren't going to be the top racers in the world," he admits. And by the same token, he "didn't want to train and didn't care so much about it." They had alternative plans.

"We realized the magazines needed something to write about," he says, "so it was an easy sell to do stories on any place we traveled to." Burt secured a list of photographers from *Powder* magazine and proceeded to work with as many as he could. During the 1987–88 season, the publishers of *Powder* were launching *Snowboarder* magazine, "and [snowboarding] was on the list of things for the photographers to shoot," he says. "So the first year *Snowboarder* came out, you pretty much saw Avalanche Snowboards everywhere, because we pumped the photographers and no one else had figured that out. That's kind of what started our thing of not racing and moving into freeriding."

Entering his last mainstream competition in 1991 at the World Cup in Japan, Burt "tied for fifth in the world in the halfpipe," he notes, hinting at how odd that statement sounds coming from him. Later that year, he and Zellers made a bid for the first-ever snowboard descent of Mount McKinley. Having spent a month honing their mountaineering skills on Alaska's Ruth Glacier in 1989, they'd glimpsed the vast possibilities of big-mountain riding.

"We went up to ride the Orient Express," he says, referring to a route that's nicknamed for the large number of Asian climbers who have fallen from the ridgeline at 19,000 feet and plummeted down a 4,000 foot headwall to their deaths. "We could have gone to the summit, but we decided that it was

// **OPPOSITE:** Launching some respectable air in 1989 at Squaw Valley's first contest. // **FOLLOWING SPREAD:** Tom Burt's landmark first descent of Cordova Peak in Valdez, Alaska. After pausing slightly to let his slough go by, Burt charges into the most dangerous and exposed section near the bergshrund at the bottom. No one has attempted this peak since, but it's not for lack of interest.

// **OPPOSITE:** With more shooting experience than anyone in snowboarding, Burt knows exactly the type of shot photographers look for.

steep and hard on the top, and we didn't know how much energy it was gonna take to ski down." Unlike many other big mountains, McKinley offers an uninterrupted 13,000 vertical-foot run down the Orient. "So we made the conscious decision to turn around wherever the fun stops," he says, staying true to Ricketts's first principle. "We weren't there to mountaineer, necessarily," he admits. "It's nice to go to the summit, but it's not our number one priority. Our number one priority is to have fun on our snowboards. Summiting is not driving us. It's snowboarding."

//

"Tom Burt is like the renaissance man of snowboarding," says Tom Hsieh. "When Tom decided to walk away from the competitive side of snowboarding and strike out on his own and bring adventure back to snowboarding, it was a radical departure because [competitions were] where money was, where sponsorship ended up being, where access to media happened to be. He left a lot on the table, but he did it for something. I think he was banking on a better future in terms of what he wanted out of snowboarding, which was to ride the best powder in the world." As it turns out, much of that happens to be in Alaska.

Burt dodged the competitive spotlight, but ended up showcasing his big terrain skills for the camera, and more often than not, Mike Hatchett was looking through the viewfinder. The founder of Tahoe-based Standard Films, Hatchett's *Totally Board* series captured the best of freeriding and freestyle throughout the '90s. As a freerider himself, Hatchett's personal passion is for shooting the big-mountain line—especially when Tom Burt is the one putting it down.

"Tom has some of the best board control I've ever seen," Hatchett says. "He just flies over blind rows, where most people wouldn't remember what was there when they saw it from the ground." By starring in snowboard films, Burt perpetuated his sponsorships and cultivated new ones, but it was never about portraying the rock-star image. "He's the raddest guy out there," Hatchett asserts, "but in a totally unorthodox way as far as his style and what he cares about. He wasn't going to change his white Vaurnet sunglasses and tight North Face outfit for anybody. That's just what he liked to wear."

In 1996, Burt set the bar for big-mountain lines in Alaska with a first descent on Cordova Peak, just outside Valdez, and Standard Films was there. "We had looked at it the whole season," Hatchett remembers, "and then finally, the one day that it was right, he did it." Hatchett describes the sixty-degree slope as "super exposed with huge crevasses and gaping holes in the middle of the run." In other words, there was zero room for error. After dropping in on the top section, Burt stopped to let his slough go by, and then proceeded to ride the more technical lower section to the bottom. "There was one crux section in the middle where, if you fall, you're dead, for sure. You just tumble into a hole or off a cliff," Hatchett says with no exaggeration whatsoever. What made it a landmark descent in Hatchett's book, though, wasn't the difficulty alone but how Burt handled it. Unlike his European counterparts, who "use ice axes and take hours to check their way down these things," explains Hatchett, Burt "flowed down the whole thing in like ten minutes." And this is what makes his style of big-mountain riding so visually appealing. "He takes lines that are really gnarly and also rides them really fast. No one wants to watch a guy stop. They want to watch him fly."

To this day, no one else has ridden Cordova, but it's not for lack of interest. "That was the only day it's been doable since then," Tom says, referring to the snow conditions and other factors necessary to pull it off. "But they look at it all the time."

//

The second morning of my trip reveals clear blue skies. There's no question—we're flying. A palpable stoke can be felt at 33 Mile, where Sean Dog orchestrates guides, pilots, film crews, clients, and various bro-down hopefuls with the deftness of a chief executive. To look at him, though, he's more like a circus ringleader. Wielding a clipboard, he's donned a Russian military hat (complete with the furry ear flaps) and Hawaiian board shorts over sweat pants. This is our fearless leader.

Burt boards a helicopter with filmmaker Justin Hostenyk and the crew from Absinthe Films;

// Tom Burt with his daughter, Nina, in 2003.

recently, Burt's become more of a big-mountain chaperone. "[Film crews] ask if I can guide with them because they know I can get down things," he says. "I can get to them if something goes wrong. I can make my way down the most rowdy line that they can. Also, they film me if there are lines left to do. So it works out alright. But more importantly for the athletes, they feel more comfortable with me there."

Tom's also become a father in the past couple years with long-time partner Tricia Maloney. So, I wonder, is there more to consider—more second guessing and a little more prudence, perhaps—when it comes to riding in the backcountry?

"To say that what I do is the most dangerous aspect of snowboarding . . . well, it's a relative thing," he says, subtly defending his choices, "because of ability, training, and experience." When I ask about his personal experience with avalanches, I'm surprised to learn that the only time he's ever been caught in one was at Squaw Valley. "When you're in bounds, you kind of let your guard down; you expect it to be safe," he says. "I got tumbled and taken under, but I ended up on top, about tip deep with my head out, so it worked out alright."

Based on this, you either conclude that snowboarding is not safe or that risk can be managed. "You don't go out and try to kill yourself," he says of life in general and big-mountain riding in particular. "But there's always a chance to die, even when you're driving. You can't tell completely that a slope is safe; you never can. Just like getting into a car, you can't tell whether someone's gonna run into you; otherwise you wouldn't get into the car that day. You know there are risks and hopefully you'll see the car coming so you can avoid it. You're always taking a chance no matter what. But does that mean you stay home and don't go out in the mountains? I'd rather live life than not live life and sit home and be scared all the time." Besides, sitting at home is just no fun. **//**

>MOUNTAIN MOTHER

In the last five years, the women of snowboarding have attracted increased coverage in both snowboarding and mainstream media. In 2000, women represented twenty-six percent of all U.S. snowboarders; by 2003, that number grew to more than thirty-four percent. Nearly every board, boot, and binding manufacturer offers models for women, designed for the female anatomy with different graphics and a more feminine color palette. Many pro women have signature models; there's an industry segment dedicated to women's snowboard clothing, and Primedia's *Surf, Snow, Skate Girl* magazine covers the sport from a female perspective.

Today, male and female riders represent snowboarding side-by-side, but make no mistake, women's place in a sport and industry largely dominated by the guys has not come without critical early female influences.

The first women of snowboarding inspired a generation of their peers to shred like a lady. Bonnie Leary Zellers, the wife of Jim Zellers, kept up with her husband and his partner in crime Tom Burt on their big mountain adventures. She chronicled their many first descents in Alaska and other remote locations, acting as both explorer and author. Julie Zell of Jackson Hole, Wyoming, pioneered big-mountain riding, winning the Queen of the Hill extreme contest three times in a row. Shannon Dunn, a Burton Global Team Rider from Southern California, started competing in the late '80s; in 1998, she won an Olympic bronze medal for the United States in Nagano, Japan. Michele Taggart packed her skis away in 1988, first trying snowboarding with her brother at Mount Bachelor, Oregon. She went on to become the winningest female rider in competition history, both in alpine and freestyle. Freeriding film star Victoria Jealouse has proven that you don't have to compete to get recognition. Today, these women are still killing it, and a new generation is on the scene. Going bigger than ever thought possible "by a girl," Kelly Clark won the gold medal in the halfpipe at the 2002 Olympics in Salt Lake City, Utah, and continues to dominate, claiming the U.S. Open halfpipe victory in 2004.

The women of professional snowboarding represent a sisterhood of sorts. Advancing the women's snowboarding movement has engendered a "we're all in this together" mentality. This type of thinking extended beyond the sport into more general and serious issues in 1996 when a group of women, including several pro women snowboarders, founded Boarding for Breast Cancer, a non-profit charity that holds a yearly benefit concert and snowboarding exhibition. This was spearheaded in large part by the efforts of Tina Basich, a woman who's often referred to as the godmother of snowboarding for her pioneering—even maternal—role in building a foundation for women's place in this sport. **//**

// **OPPOSITE:** Bonnie Leary Zellers gets some freshies in Nevada's Mount Rose backcountry in 1988. // **LEFT:** A resident of Whistler, British Columbia, Victoria Jealouse is snowboarding's sweetheart. She's one of the few women to make a lasting and successful career as a freerider, starring in countless films from a number of different film companies.

Tina Basich has some travel advice. It's not where to go or what to do, though she could certainly help plan a trip to anywhere it snows. This pioneer snowboarder has traveled the world for nearly twenty years as a sponsored professional, making snowboard films and competing at the highest level. Along the way, she's learned a thing or two about traveling. // For one, lose the hotel bedspreads and stash them in the closet. Hotels don't wash those, and you have no idea (though you can guess) what they've been through. Next, if you don't bring a pillowcase, use a T-shirt. Sure, hotels wash those, but you want your cheeks against your own fabric. And when it comes to eating out, it's nice to have a personal set of chopsticks in lieu of not-so-clean silverware from the dodgier restaurants. Tina's are Mickey Mouse brand from Disneyland Tokyo, but any will do. // The veteran snowboarder also has a few caveats with regard to backcountry snowboarding, particularly on the unforgiving peaks of Alaska: Always determine your safe zones before dropping in. Always ride one at a time, and wear an avalanche beacon. Follow these rules and you might not get caught in an avalanche. And if you do, you just might survive. // In this eclectic collection of motherly advice—hygiene tips alongside pointers for not getting yourself killed—we find the spirit of Tina Basich. She's been dubbed the "Godmother of Snowboarding" for her enduring contribution to the sport; however, this open designation goes beyond a mere label. Basich is like a Donna Reed of action sports, looking after friends and family with a decidedly maternal approach. At thirty-six years old she might not have kids, but she's nurtured the sport of snowboarding from a very early stage. She made sacrifices to always be there. She reaped

// OPPOSITE: Tina Basich hiking for freshies in the Utah backcountry.

the rewards of its success and is proud of how it's matured into adulthood. Make no mistake, though, Basich is no June Cleaver. She's responsible for elevating the sport overall and for women in particular, bagging numerous titles and first descents along the way. With her maternal instincts come the fierce will to succeed and a natural impulse to defend women's place in snowboarding. But first she had to leave home.

//

Seventeen-year-old Tina Basich stood atop the halfpipe of the 1987 World Championships in Breckenridge, Colorado, and watched the other women—her competition—take their runs. She was up next, and the halfpipe seemed huge. It was much bigger than the one she was used to at Donner Ski Ranch. "There's no way I can try my ally-oop in a pipe this big," she thought, as the nerves settled around her stomach. But she had a decent bag of tricks and a string of first-place finishes from local Tahoe competitions. Most of all, she had nothing to lose.

This was the attitude in those early days of snowboarding. Basich discovered the sport in 1985 when she hiked for her first turns on a rented board [because they didn't yet allow snowboarders on the lifts] at Soda Springs ski resort. Finding it came easy, she embraced snowboarding as both an athletic and social outlet, furthering her search for identity at a crucial point in her teenage years. Without pretense or precedent, the semi-secret sport of snowboarding became a diary in which she recorded her history.

Basich dropped into the Breckenridge halfpipe only two years later. A series of method airs and frontside indies netted her a sixth-place finish. Not bad—sixth in the world. On her first trip away from home, away from the Sacramento, California, suburbs where she'd grown up, Tina Basich set a new course for her life, one that lead to more travel and snowboarding than she ever thought possible.

In 1988, after a second appearance at the Worlds and another sixth-place finish, the newly formed Kemper Snowboards recruited her as its sole woman snowboarder. She graduated from high school. A salary of $250 per month and a small travel budget were enough for her to defer college and turn down an art scholarship. After all, she'd become a professional snowboarder.

As a *de facto* pioneer in women's snowboarding, Basich felt responsibilities beyond those of her contractual obligations. "I had to ride and do well in competitions and be in photo shoots not just for myself," she wrote in her 2003 autobiography, *Pretty Good for a Girl*, "but so girls would see this sport and it wouldn't fade for them or take a backseat to guys." Guys such as her Kemper teammates Andy Hetzel and Matt Goodman may have been driving the sport, but Basich was right there riding shotgun. "It was all I could do to keep up," she described, "but hell if I wasn't going to try. I rode

// **LEFT:** At a pipe contest in 1989 at Boreal Ridge, California. // **RIGHT:** In the early days, Tina tried her hand at snowboard racing as well.

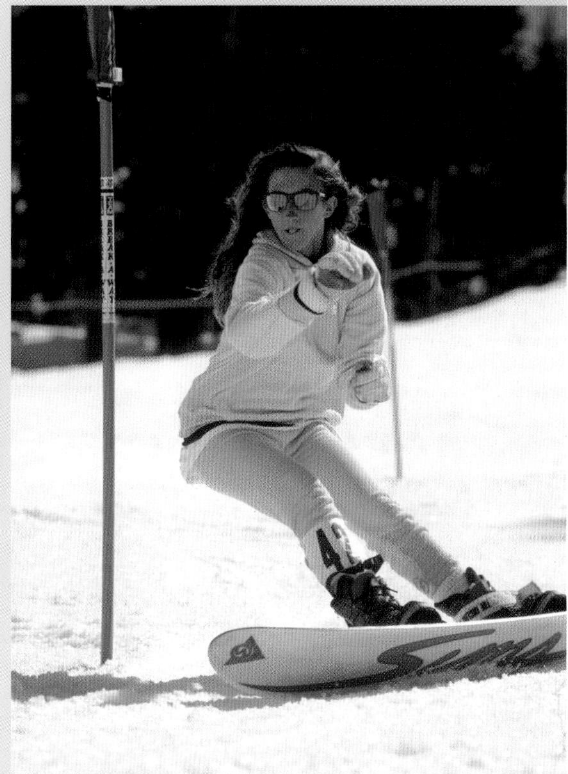

harder and even started to jump cliffs because I had to get the girl shot for the team."

In 1990, at age twenty-one, Basich and the Kemper team relocated to Utah, according to the state license plates, the land of "The Greatest Snow on Earth." It was the place she'd call home for the next decade, the place she'd go when not traveling to events and photo shoots in Europe, Japan, or New Zealand. That first year she competed in fifteen major competitions, winning the national halfpipe championship at the U.S. Open and a second place overall. For the next three years, she went on a tear of top-three finishes, including a second at the King of the Hill extreme-snowboarding contest in Alaska. Even as one of the senior members of snowboarding's swelling professional ranks, the door to Basich's home was always open. "My house in Utah was big enough to fit all of my snowboarding friends," she writes. "When it snowed, people would just show up. People knew where my Hide-A-Key was and I welcomed friends anytime."

One of those people was her younger brother, Michael, who learned to snowboard alongside Tina on that fateful day in 1985. He eventually turned pro and began competing as well, but only after recovering from the epilepsy he developed when he was nine and Tina, thirteen. Due to the epilepsy, the family decided to take Michael out of school, and Tina, being the big sister, put Michael before everything else and devoted her time to doing art and woodworking projects with him at home. It's essentially how they communicated. "I'd try to be there for him

// Basich at home in Utah with her friend, Blue Montgomery, 1996.

in his world, and if Michael wanted to build a fort out of the branches in the backyard, I instantly made that my whole world."

It took three years for him to overcome the epilepsy, to start using his voice again, and return to school full-time. The experience solidified the life philosophies to which Basich now subscribes. "He's always reminded me to live life to the fullest because he's true to himself and looks beyond the normal path, creating new ideas and adventures for both of us. He taught me the simple mind-set of not needing a reason to be happy and loving unconditionally for the moment that you're in."

Mike Basich has enjoyed a fruitful career as a pro snowboarder in the realm of competition as well as freeriding. His crafty, artistic background led to the construction of a sixty-foot-long, seventeen-foot-high rainbow rail that he was towed into by a snowmobile. The following season, he coordinated a 120-foot drop from a helicopter onto a steep Alaskan face. In both instances, he somehow managed to set up a camera on a tripod and, via remote control, shoot photos of himself. Both of the stunning images appeared in countless magazines throughout American and Japanese snowboarding magazines.

"Being the older sister and starting on the World Cup of snowboarding right out of high school, at first I felt like I was leading Michael through our snowboarding careers," she says. "But I soon

// **ABOVE:** Tina and Mike on a heli-boarding mission with the Wasatch Powderbird guides. // **RIGHT:** Sister and brother confer at a contest.

realized what a leader he was for me also. Many times I looked to him for advice and guidance for the next step. He is the first person I would turn to out in the backcountry or on a photo shoot when I was unsure of my snowboarding and needed help to push through challenges. He is such a leader in a quiet way, and he amazes me."

//

The television set was scarcely present in the Basich living room when Tina was growing up, but in 1976, it emerged from the closet on the occasion of the Summer Olympics in Montreal, Canada. Romanian gymnast Nadia Comaneci nailed a perfect score, winning the gold medal and inspiring young female athletes the world over. Tina was one of them.

By 1994, Tina had established herself as one of the top female snowboarders in the world. She and long-time friend Shannon Dunn each came out with the first women's signature snowboards that year with Kemper and Sims respectively. Designed to their own specifications as female riders, women would no longer have to adapt to men's gear. Tina and Shannon also collaborated with Swag Clothing to launch the Prom line, "allowing us the freedom to design clothes with slimmer cuts, pastel colors, and butterfly logos," she writes. "We were as girly as we wanted to be and rocked it with confidence." Bridging the gap in performance levels between men and women, though, would take a more concerted effort.

Until then, women's competitions took a back seat to the men's. For the most part, women's riding styles didn't have the explosive appeal. At many events, a women's category wasn't even offered, especially at big air contests where the jumps were so massive few thought women could clear them. The 1994 Air & Style Big Air in Innsbruck, Austria, was one such event. After challenging the "no girls allowed" rule, Tina and Shannon cleared the sixty-foot gap jump in front of 15,000 people. Though they weren't officially judged, "magazine articles later reported that we'd gone bigger than some of the guys," she writes, "and probably would have placed in the top ten."

When the Winter X-Games emerged two years later, it embraced the women's division and made zero concessions. In other words, there were no ladies' tees. "Sixteen girls entered the big-air contest that year," she writes, "but when it came down to the day of competition, only four of us showed up. It was risky and dangerous—a fifty-foot jump with snow conditions that were icy and firm. It was completely sketchy and scared off most of the competitive field." With the world watching—110 million viewers—Basich and her fellow competitors felt an obligation to represent for their gender. "We couldn't back out," she writes, "because we had to have a girls division." Pulling a reserved backside 360, Basich got third. It was a great victory in the battle for equal recognition.

The peak of Basich's snowboarding career doubled as the peak of women's snowboarding at

// OPPOSITE: A smooth method air in New Zealand, 1995.

// OPPOSITE: The magic touch.

the time. The Winter X-Games had become a pop-culture phenomenon by its third year, and had put snowboarding squarely in the sights of mainstream America. Meanwhile, Basich concentrated on perfecting a new big-air trick that was certain to warrant, and simultaneously seal, her place in snowboarding and women's sports history. When the time came and the cameras rolled, she launched the sixty-foot gap and stuck, for the first time in women's competitive snowboarding, a backside 720. She bagged the win.

Wearing the gold medal around her neck, she noted that, "even a few pro snowboarder guys came up and told me they couldn't do that trick yet." That year, a total of 6,700 of her pro model snowboards were sold around the world—6,700 women inspired to make snowboarding their own. Of Tina Basich's many accomplishments and contributions, though, one transcends the relative triviality of sport, glory, and achievement like no other.

Basich and many of her friends received a wake-up call in 1995 when they learned a colleague, twenty-six-year-old Monica Steward, was battling breast cancer. A cofounder of Bonfire snowboard clothing and close friend of pro snowboarder Michelle Taggart, Steward endured a mastectomy and fought the cancer into remission. A group of friends, including Taggart and Shannon Dunn, decided to organize a snowboarding event to benefit breast cancer research and awareness. Boarding for Breast Cancer (B4BC) was born.

The inaugural event debuted in 1996 at Sierra-at-Tahoe resort in Northern California. The Beastie Boys played to 5,600 fans and B4BC supporters. A group of 120 pro riders, including Shaun Palmer, competed in an exhibition-style contest, "throwing down their best moves in the halfpipe and big air," Basich writes. In honor of their friend Monica, who had succumbed to a relapse three months earlier and died tragically at the age of twenty-nine, the organization raised $50,000. Since then, the non-profit foundation has generated more than $1 million for the cause.

Now retired from competition, Tina Basich continues to ride and continues to nurture. She's moved back to Tahoe, closer to her family and to where it all began. She hosts a show called *GKA* (Girls Kick Ass) on Fox's FUEL network. "It's a girl's action-sports show," she explains, "that showcases all the great female athletes in snowboarding, skateboarding, surfing, motocross, and things like that." Such primetime attention is proof that the once infant sport of snowboarding is all grown up. But that doesn't mean it—or you—are exempt from some good motherly advice: "When you're flying in an airplane and you get up from your seat," she admonishes, "don't grab the seat in front of you. There's nothing worse than trying to sleep and someone's jarring your seat to get up, so be courteous of other people."

Yes, Tina. ***//***

>THE COMPETITIVE ASPECT: **DRIVING THE SPORT**

In snowboarding's purest form, rules are imposed by Nature alone, and boundaries are self-imposed. To ride purely is to never reach the finish line and never be judged. But if snowboarding is not competitive in essence, then it is by necessity, driven by its will to thrive as a world-class sport and as a global industry. Competition fueled snowboarding's meteoric growth from the back hills of Vermont and California to the world stage in comparatively little time and legitimized what many labeled as a passing fad.

During the late 1960s and into the '70s, Americans on their Snurfers held go-for-broke downhill races on what amounted to a kid's toy. In 1982, promoter Paul Graves bridged the gap between Snurfing and snowboarding with the National Snowsurfing Championships in Woodstock, Vermont, where both types of boards were used. A year later, Jake Burton Carpenter and Tom Sims held back-to-back championship events—the Nationals in Vermont and the Worlds in California—launching the modern era of snowboard competition.

These early contests were as much about getting snowboarders together in the same place as they were about pitting one person's mettle against another. They were festivals to celebrate this thing that only a handful of people knew about. There was no money and the prestige of winning didn't extend far beyond your peers. Downhill and slalom comprised the first two disciplines, borrowing heavily from alpine skiing. After all, the events were held at ski resorts on slopes where, previously, only skiers raced. One event—a downhill race—stands out, however, as unique to snowboarding, for it took place inside a natural, snow-covered wave.

Washington State's Mount Baker embraced the sport like few others in the early 1980s. Home to Craig Kelly and the Mount Baker Hard Core (MBHC), it is known for harsh weather, great terrain, and well-heeled riders. A man named Bob Barci conceived a slalom race where racers would charge down a natural gully, a large halfpipe of sorts, with gates positioned high on the walls. In what became the Legendary Mount Baker Banked Slalom, riders arc turns as if slapping the lip of a motionless wave, frontside and backside all the way to the finish. Over the years, the race has achieved cult status. It receives little or no press; there's no cash to be won, and it won't earn you points of any kind. Yet top snowboarders from multiple countries and representing every era consistently turn up to this event which celebrated its twentieth anniversary in 2004. They race for fun and for what a Banked Slalom title means within the tribe. They show up to reconnect with an element of snowboard culture that's arguably been lost to progress and commercialism on the world stage.

// Mount Baker, the Northwest snowboarding Mecca on a powder day in 1993.

The International Snowboarding Federation (ISF) formed in 1991 as the sport's governing body, and in 1993, it hosted the first official Snowboard World Championships in Ischgl, Austria. Around this same time, a small group of hardcore riders in Alaska conceived of an entirely fresh idea: The World Extreme Snowboard Championships. Pioneered in 1992 and reborn as The King of the Hill in '94, this event was designed as a way for the top freeride and big-mountain riders to showcase

// ABOVE: Left to Right: Terry Kidwell, Bob Klein, and Tom Sims at the first inaugural Mount Baker Banked Slalom in 1985. Like most other events of the day, Sims won. **// RIGHT:** A view down the course of the most famous slalom event in snowboarding history.

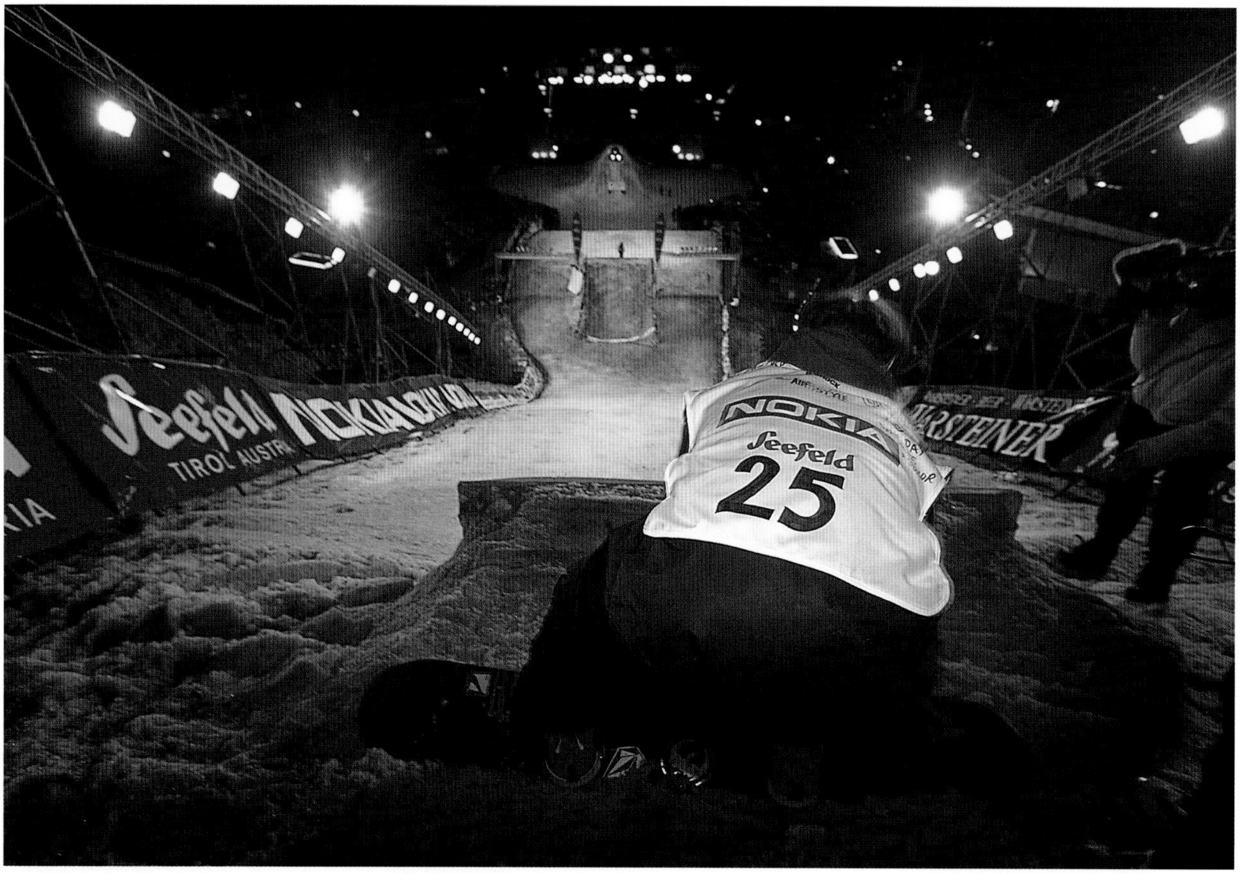
Seefeld
NOKIA
Seefeld
25

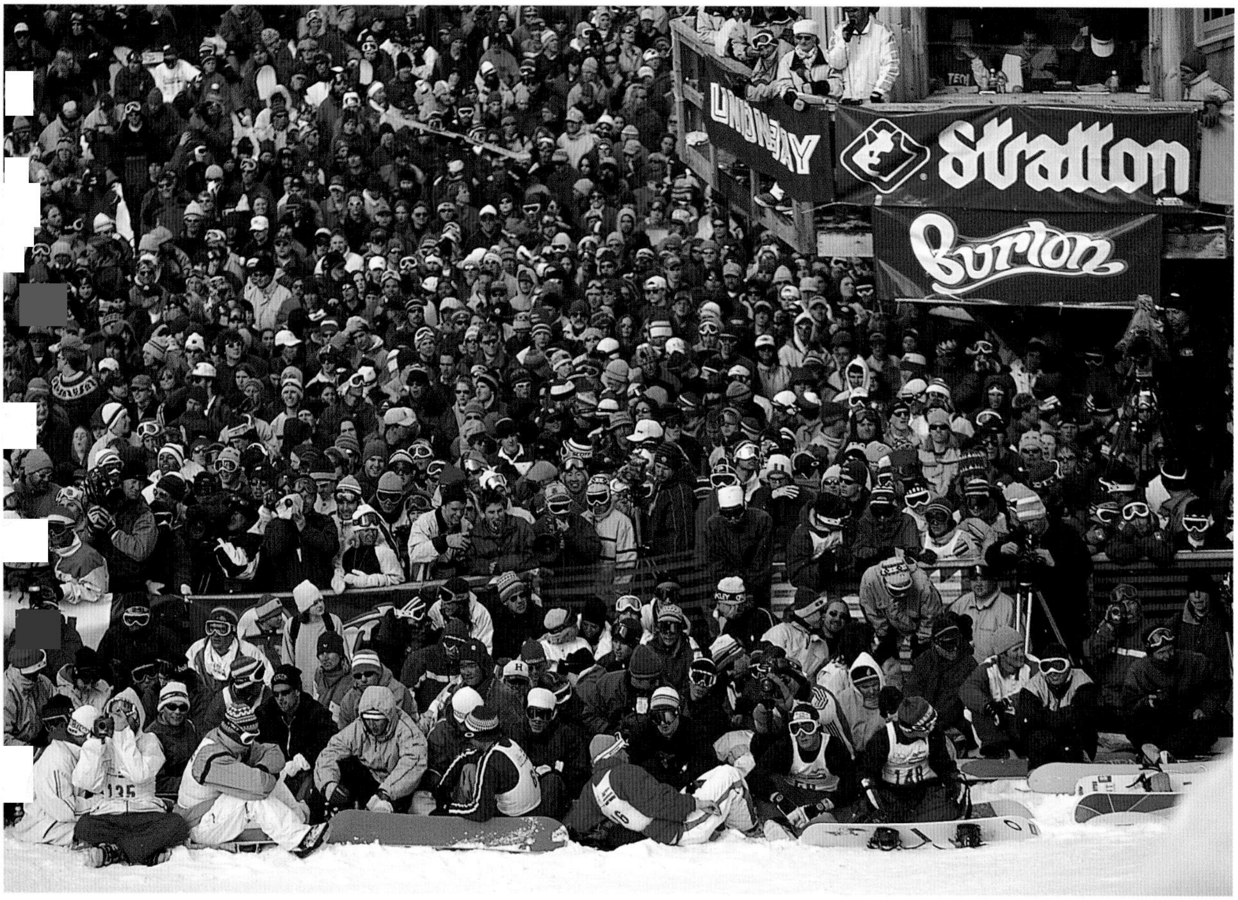
Stratton
Burton

// **OPPOSITE, TOP:** Tina Basich stares down the barrel of victory at a Big Air contest in Austria, 1995. // **BOTTOM:** The teeming throngs at the U.S. Open, 1996.

their skills in the backcountry. Helicopters were required to access the venue, and very little about the event could be controlled or predicted. First was a timed downhill run that dropped 4,000 feet; next was a 3,000-vertical-foot freestyle run judged for style. The last and most extreme section pitted riders against a steep, 4,000 vertical-foot face characterized by cliffs, couloirs, and cornices; whoever rode the most difficult line and made it look good won. As much as the King of the Hill captured snowboarding's essence, it exploited the purity of freeriding by corralling it into a competition. It was last held in 1999.

For a number of competitive formats that blossomed in the 1990s, it's tough to tell which came first, the discipline itself or the television coverage that popularized them. Boardercross, slopestyle, and big air lend themselves to television like reality TV. They are spectacular to watch, and you're more or less guaranteed to see someone crash. Boardercross borrows from dirt bike racing, pitting four to six riders against one another on a slalom course. Slopestyle is like the street version of skateboarding (with distant roots in the gymnastic floor routine). A single rider performs through a snowboard park, using jumps and other obstacles for launching airs and doing technical tricks. Big Air is similar, but it's a one-shot deal—he or she who goes biggest and pulls the best trick ends up with the big cardboard check.

At one time or another, each of the pioneers and players in snowboarding's history measured him or herself in a competitive forum. For a while, it was the only way to make a living in the sport. One needed to compete now and then, to the benefit of sponsors, in order to freeride the rest of the time. These days, most riders specialize in a single discipline because competition has become so fierce. It got that way, in part, from the intensity and drive of a kid once known as "Mini Shred." Most now know him as "The Palm," a.k.a. Shaun Palmer, a name that is synonymous with snowboarding's competitive spirit. **//**

Shaun Palmer Pro Snowboarder 2, a video game modeled after the five-time World Snowboarding Champion, grants 3D-motion-graphic access to the sport's most colorful character. Controller in hand, you *are* Shaun Palmer. You ride with great purpose and reckless abandon. You ride bare-chested with a punk-rock soundtrack cranking in the background. After dominating the Tahoe scene—home-turf resorts like Donner Ski Ranch, Heavenly, and Squaw Valley—you tour the national and international circuit. You compete, quickly advancing through the levels of difficulty and prestige. Your simple and straightforward objective is to stomp the competition and win. The game is professional snowboarding, and you're quite possibly the best who's ever played. // Released in 2002, the video game capitalized on Palmer's storied twenty-year career and the tremendous level of fame he'd achieved. Driven by snowboarding's overall popularity, the game features other top snowboarders including Olympic halfpipe gold medalist Ross Powers and freestyle diva Tara Dakides. But none of them—no other snowboarder, for that matter—can match Palmer's mass-market appeal. In his day, he was the marquise brand, a household name of sorts. He was the guy *USA Today* dubbed the "World's Greatest Athlete." // In May of 1998, the page-one headline landed on newsstands and breakfast tables throughout America, crowning the new king of sports. Though certainly debatable, especially considering the source, Palmer for one was thoroughly convinced. Two years earlier, the snowboard champion had added downhill mountain biking to his budding portfolio of professional sports. Riding as a relative unknown, he won a world slalom championship and missed

// **OPPOSITE:** The man, the name, the brand.

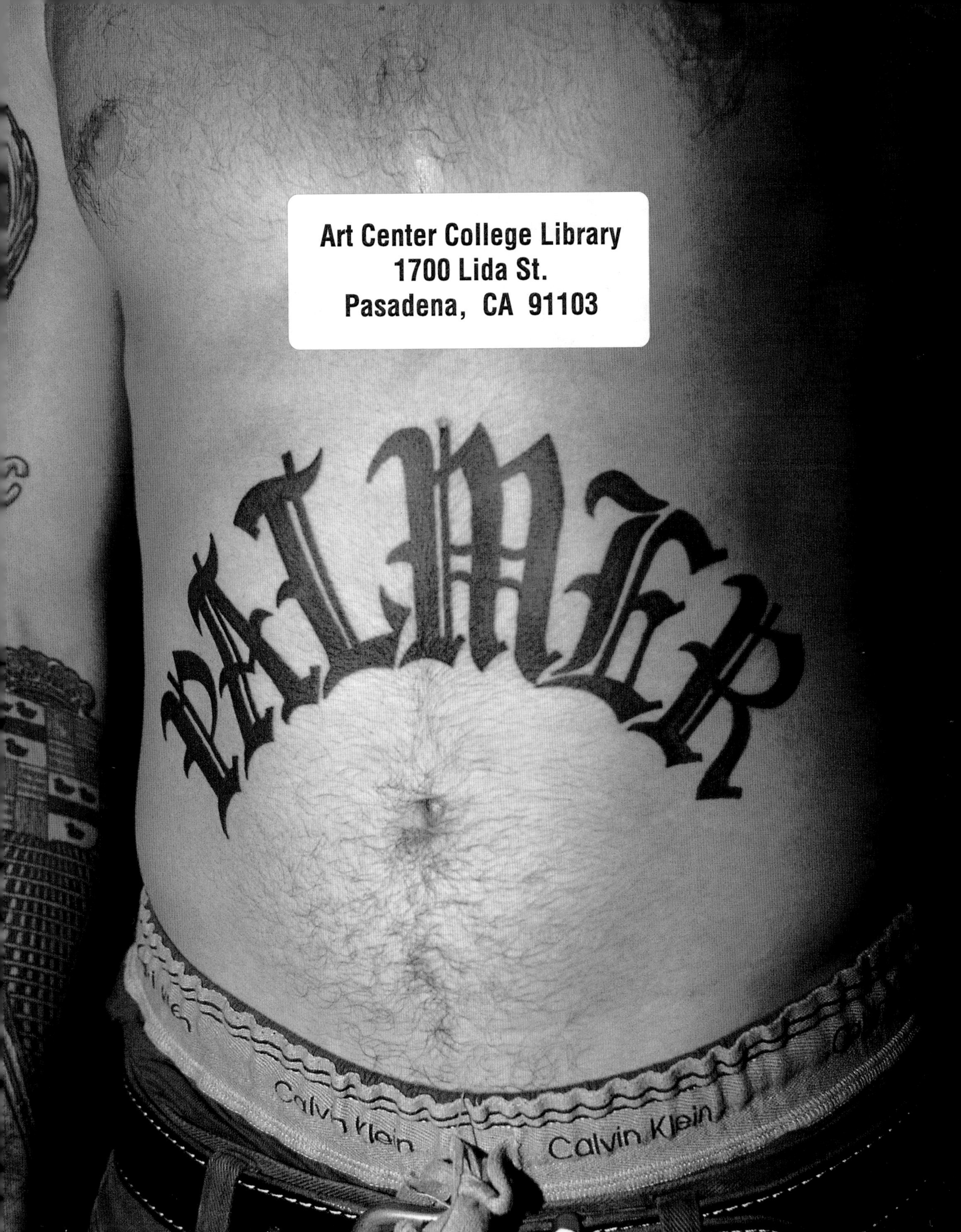

Art Center College Library
1700 Lida St.
Pasadena, CA 91103

the downhill title by fifteen-hundredths of a second. He then signed the most lucrative sponsorship deal in the sport's brief history. The following year, he qualified for a Supercross main event, ranking him in the crème de la crème of dirt-bike racing. Drawing obvious comparisons to crossover jocks like Bo Jackson and Deion Sanders, the article described twenty-nine-year-old Palmer as "175 pounds of cocky sinew and scar tissue seemingly held together by tattoos." The brash-yet-supremely-talented phenomenon signaled the arrival, at least to those unfamiliar with snowboarding and mountain biking, of a new athletic breed. Palmer put a face on action sports. The expression, which spoke volumes, amounted to an arrogant snarl.

Self-styled from the very beginning, Palmer fashioned an image for himself that meshed rock-star belligerence with supernatural athleticism. "He helped define the delinquent ethos of alternative sports," wrote Rob Buchanan in 1997, "mostly through his off-the-course style: flamingly rude and crude, with a devotion to the black arts of partying." In many ways, Palmer was conscious of his actions—when he was in a conscious state, that is—and the consequences that followed. For the most part, aside from hangovers and the occasional black eye, his antics netted a positive gain. If Palmer picked a fight for no reason or trashed a hotel room, it just further cemented his status as the asshole who took winning for granted. He played this game, like any other, to win. It was all a contest for him. Just winners and losers. Like in the video game, according to a strategy guide, "Each level has a certain number of goals or challenges. In each level you collect local sponsors, collect the secret sponsor, accumulate points, and smash something." By and large, that's the Palmer method. You meet the challenges and win titles. Sponsors set you up, and you cash oversized checks for tens of thousands of dollars in contest winnings. And whether or not you win or lose, something (or someone) has to get smashed. But this behavior wasn't completely under Palmer's control. He couldn't help but to act out because he was pissed. The World's Greatest Athlete had issues.

//

Born in San Diego, California, on November 14, 1968, Shaun Palmer took one on the chin before he was old enough to remember it. His father, a construction worker, bailed only months after his birth, leaving him to be raised by his mother, Jana. From childhood, the two butted heads. Shaun bitterly rejected any male figure who entered the picture, no doubt giving the youngster a head start on his vibing techniques.

In 1976, Jana packed up and moved the two of them to South Lake Tahoe, where they could be closer to Shaun's maternal grandmother, Perky Neely. Working as a waitress at Harrah's casino, she'd end up raising Shaun more so than his mother. It just seemed to work better than living with Jana and his stepfather. Perky also had "lots

// **CLOCKWISE FROM LEFT:** Young Palmer flashing a cocksure smile for the camera at the Worlds in 1985. // Celebrating his first World title four years later in 1989. // Cutting it up with Mike Ranquet at the 1988 *ISM* magazine board test.

of spunk." As a street-smart seven-year-old, he found himself in a ski-town environment characterized by gambling, partying, and vice in general—a recipe for disaster for many but an opportunity for young Palmer.

Lake Tahoe offered plenty of diversions for a young athlete with a limited attention span for school. Palmer preferred skiing the local mountains, most often with his childhood buddy Glen Plake, (who'd become a superstar skier in his own right) to sitting in a classroom anyday. Palmer started riding dirt bikes at age six when his mother bought him a 50-cc Honda and he played Little League as an all-star second baseman. Then he discovered skateboarding. "As soon as I did that," Palmer told Rob Buchanan, "I got into drugs. I sold weed and shit like that. I did `shrooms and coke and all that crap. That's what I did, but I did grow out of it. I kind of crawled out of that realm of people." His combined background in skiing and skateboarding, not to mention his rebellious nature, drew him to snowboarding like a moth to a flame, except that he could take the heat.

Early snowboard contraptions started showing up more frequently around Tahoe in the early 1980s. Palmer, like many others, started on the Snurfer. At age fourteen he "hiked to the top of the fuckin' sled run and went down making big fast turns with the rope on the front," he remembers. By the next season, he was working as a grunt for Avalanche Snowboards with pioneer designer Chris Sanders. He enjoyed a short-lived sponsorship by the

// Palmer en route to defeating Craig Kelly and securing his second consecutive World Championship victory in one of snowboarding's most legendary matchups.

// **LEFT:** The inverted extrovert in 1990. // **RIGHT:** On a Sims Switchblade at Squaw Valley in 1989.

company but was quickly recruited as a junior for the Sims team. Tom Sims remembers the day. The extroverted teen rode right up to him and practically demanded to be sponsored. Sims took one run with the prodigy and promptly gave him a board, starting a ten-year relationship.

Nicknamed "Mini-Shred" for both his size and style, sixteen-year-old Palmer entered his first junior pro contest in 1985 at the World Championships in Soda Springs. Sweeping the gold medals in half-pipe, slalom, and downhill, he set a precedent for excelling in multiple disciplines.

Palmer's arrival on the snowboarding scene coincided with the launch of snowboarding's first dedicated magazine. Palmer's timing, his attitude, his approach . . . it was all perfect. "He talked a big game and backed it up on a daily basis," remembers Tom Hsieh, "and that was extremely attractive to our readership. Shaun Palmer was quickly anointed as one of the rising stars of snowboarding."

Blessed with tremendous athletic ability, the junior world champ dropped out of school in the eleventh grade and continued his tear into the adult ranks. He won everything because he was good and becuase he couldn't stand to lose. "I have to win," he says. "It's in my blood stream." Palmer won the Mount Baker Banked Slalom in 1986 and 1987, its second and third inaugural years,

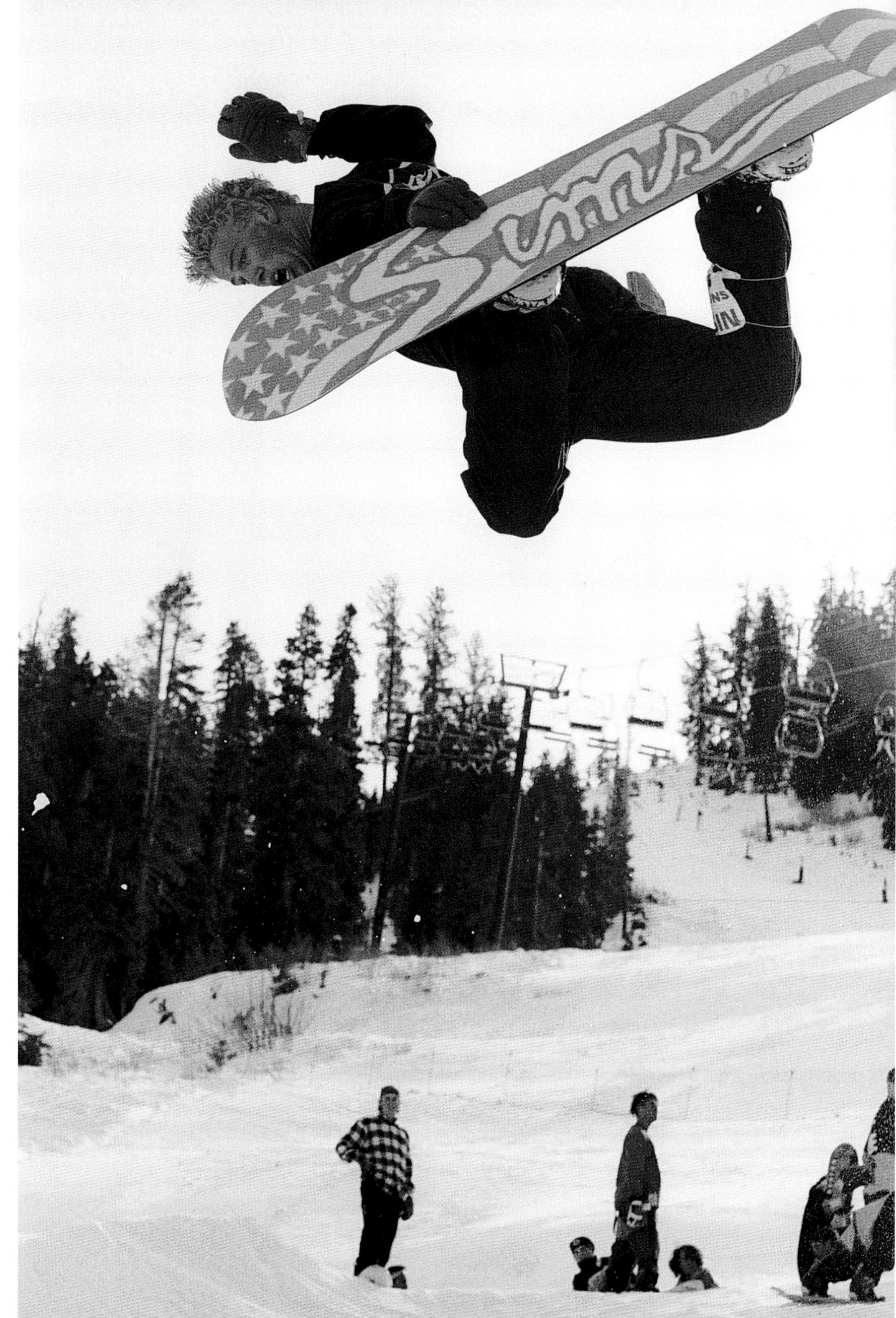

// The base of Palmer's first signature model flaunted his patriotic pride.

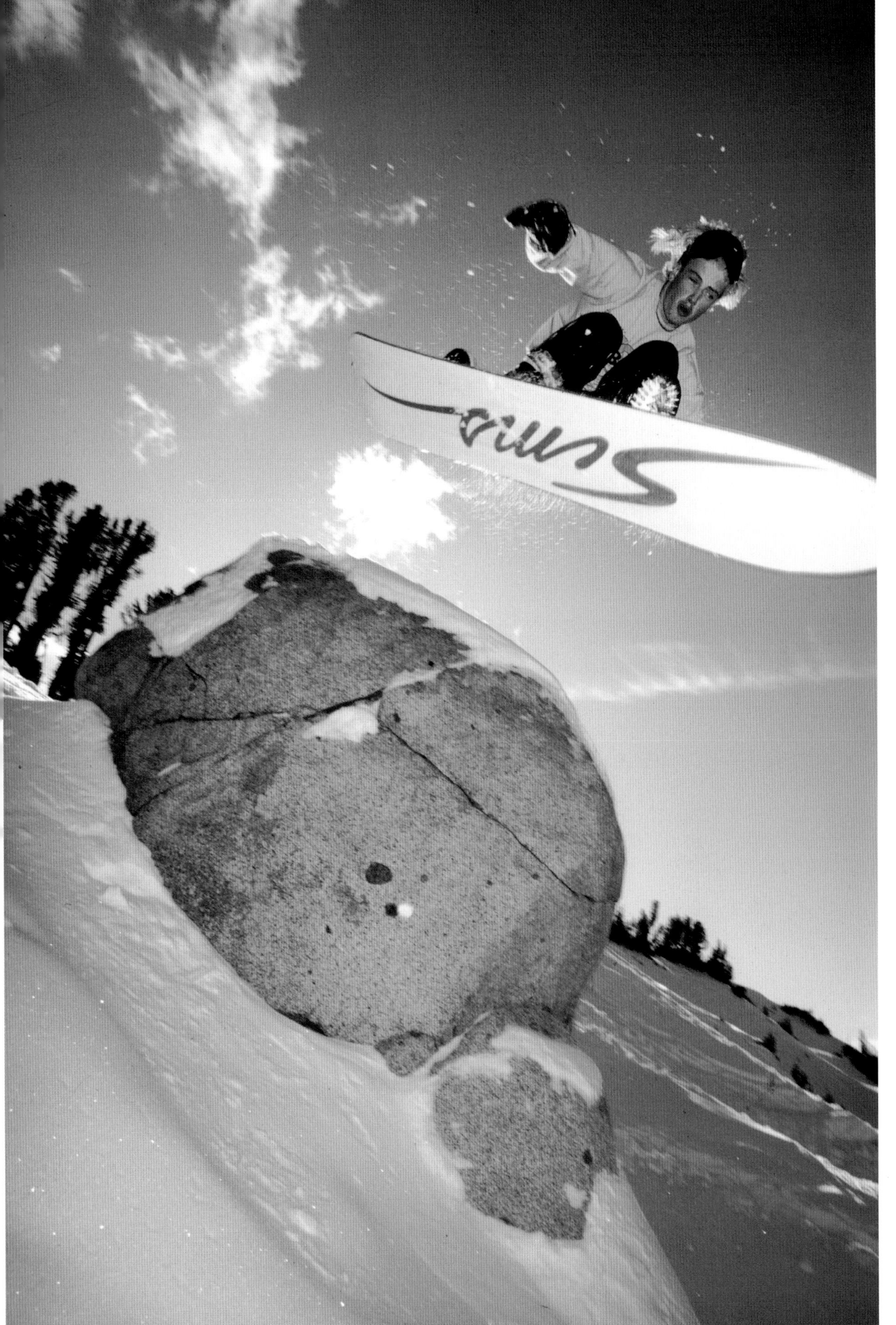

// Before the days of proper snowboard boots in 1987.

// **OPPOSITE:** Showing off his signature clown snowboard graphic in 1992, Palmer's radical choice of hair color predated Dennis Rodman by several years.

but according to Tom Sims, he wasn't the typical portrait of a champion. "Shaun shows up wearing a Santa Claus hat with a ten-foot tail and a ball on the end with baggy clothes and casually wins the race," he remembers. Most competitors at that time would have had a race suit on and would have been focused. Sims continues, "He couldn't have been more casual or having more fun. Almost treated it as a joke, and he won. A lot of his wins were like that."

Palmer's early career was nearing a climax in 1988 when, in protest, he rode straight down the center of the World Championship halfpipe. Legend has it he flipped off judges and organizers alike because he didn't think the event was up to snuff. The next year, he returned to the Worlds to face Craig Kelly in the sport's biggest showdown to date. "They moved the halfpipe up onto the mountain that year," Tina Basich remembers. "And it was the first time they built, like, tombstones at the top of the pipe." These were extensions above the lip that allowed riders to catch more air. "Shaun was sitting on his board getting ready," she says. "I went up and said, 'Good luck, Shaun.' And he's just like, 'Yeah, I'm just gonna take this thing.' So he dropped in and he took the thing. Then he got up on the podium and gave that look like, 'Of course I was gonna win.'" He returned the next year and won a second World Championship title.

"Shaun Palmer, alone, embodied the heart and soul of snowboarding," says Hsieh. "You've got this performance-driven rider who has a complete disregard for how people think of and perceive him. And that's what snowboarding started as many years ago. It was more than a sport; it was a lifestyle, it was an attitude, it was an irreverence for things that had come before us. It was something that we wanted to call our own and be individuals. And he was all that."

In 1992 Palmer's grandmother, Perky, developed cancer and died soon after, sending him into a tailspin of drinking and frustration. More than ever, he lost control. The rage that had always fueled his competitive edge went into overdrive, and he vented on whomever happened to shoot him a sideways glance. His contest results also suffered. But then again, this was a time when Jeff Brushie hit his prime and Terje Haakonsen was starting his reign. For Palmer, it was time to evolve, to channel his frustration, and perhaps broaden his range.

//

Palmer was known for talking game and backing it up. He was known for debauchery and for flaunting his patriotism. With broad recognition in the world of snowboarding and a reputation that preceded him, the Palmer name was worth something. Partnering with a Swiss investor named Jurg Kunz, he parlayed it into a snowboard company: Palmer USA Ltd. The line debuted in the spring of 1995, and the first boards were expensive, heavy, and they fell apart. Today, however, Palmer is a premier high-performance brand. Shaun maintains the

// The king returns to his throne in Solven, Austria, at the Swatch Boardercross Tour, 1997. Palmer earned countless boardercross titles and promoted his snowboard company in the process.

title of CEO, though he's more of a statesman. Day to day he still has to *be* Shaun Palmer, and that has nothing to do with balance sheets and management.

It was also at this point that Palmer decided to give mountain biking a shot. "I went out with a friend of mine, [pro mountain biker] Randy Lawrence, in Big Bear," he says. "I rode the chair up, came down, and I was hooked. Then I got a semi-decent bike and won some expert races. The following year I spent the money to fly myself around to the World Cups and Nationals, paying my own bill. I went to Italy and got seventh at the World Cup; that's what shocked everybody." Proving it wasn't a fluke, he returned to the United States and won his first National Championship Series race in Big Bear Lake, California. Punctuating this feat—and shocking the tightly wrapped world of mountain biking—Palmer climbed atop the podium wearing a gold lamé suit, one of many flashy outfits his mother made for just such occasions. Flanked by two shaved-legged also-rans dressed in logo-strewn Lycra, Palmer had officially arrived . . . again.

The Palm took to mountain biking as easily as someone picks up *Pro Snowboarder 2*, invigorating the sport in the process with his brash attitude and unique brand of charisma. After a short bidding war, he signed a three-year contract with team Specialized/Mountain Dew estimated at nearly one million dollars. Palmer traveled to national races in a forty-foot, rock-star tour bus decked in sponsor's logos and, of course, the "Palmer" insignia written in huge old-English letters—a larger version of the tattoo etched across his abdomen. He won several titles in both the downhill and slalom disciplines, but never achieved his World-Championship goal. In some ways, the competition met Palmer head-on—but his competitors were single-sport athletes that rode year-round. Palmer was simultaneously maintaing the pro snowboarding career he had never completely walked away from.

Snowboarding still was evolving at a rapid clip in the years Palmer stepped off center stage. ESPN had introduced the X-Games, and a new event known as boardercross had aggressive athletes clamoring to compete. A frenetic steeplechase-style event, it was as perfectly tailored to Palmer's skills as his mother's suits were to his five-foot-eight-inch frame. Based on a motocross format, competitors sprint through a downhill course with burmed turns, whoops, and big rollers. Elbows fly. First to the bottom wins. Having already raced pro motocross, Palmer knew the value of a holeshot, and the slalom and downhill events in the early days of snowboarding had taught him tremendous edge control. A World Champion in slalom mountain biking, he could maintain downhill momentum by flowing with the terrain. Fire up the ESPN cameras—this was Palmer's world.

"I'm going to have to retire," he boasted to viewers in 1998, "this is just getting too easy." Palmer

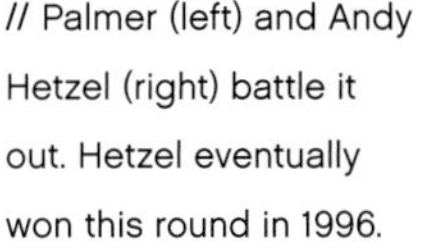

// Palmer (left) and Andy Hetzel (right) battle it out. Hetzel eventually won this round in 1996.

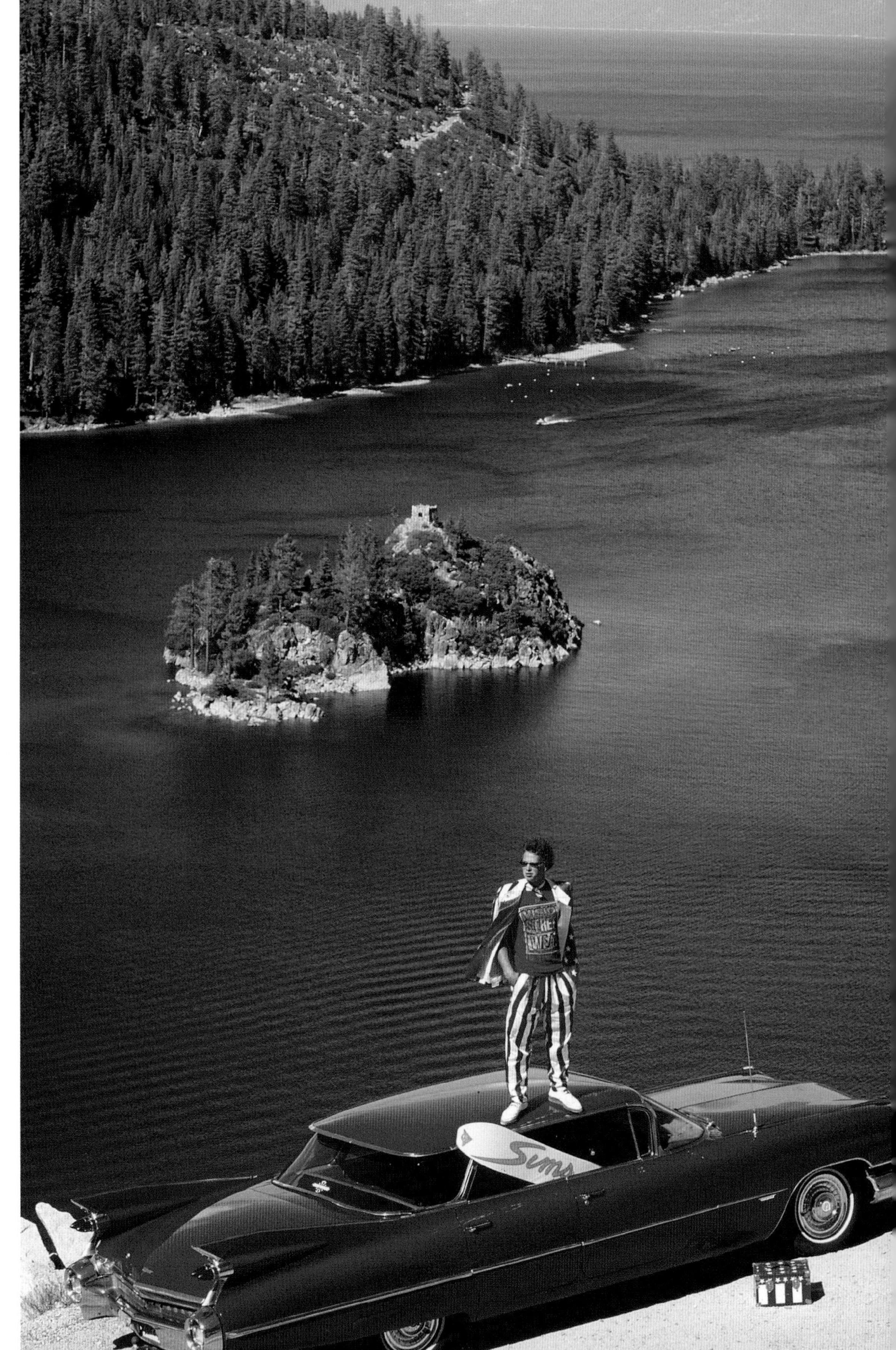

// Overlooking Emerald Bay in Lake Tahoe, California: a 1959 Cadillac, Shaun Palmer, the stars and stripes, a Sims snowboard, and brazen pride. // **OPPOSITE, CLOCKWISE FROM TOP LEFT:** On the rise in 1987 with one of his first Caddies. // Fronting for his punk rock band, Fungus, with bass player Brad Holmes in 1993. // The hairstyle that never caught on, while riding in the Utah backcountry in 1993. // At the Sims Team camp in Mount Bachelor, Oregon, Palmer wears one of several victory suits that were custom tailored for him by his mom.

won three boardercross gold medals in a row in 1997, '98, and '99. It became so easy, in fact, that in 1999 he competed in four different sports: snowboarding, snow biking, snowmobile racing, and skiing. The latter caused, perhaps, the most commotion. Having skied when he was younger, Palmer took a shot at skiercross, measuring himself against a few ex–U.S. Olympic Team members. He won the early heats but snagged a tip on the starting gate in the finals. Determined, Palmer came back in 2000 to win gold in both major skiercross events—the X-Games and the Gravity Games—by huge margins and promptly retired. "I beat the best skiers in the world twice in one year. That was enough," he told *Penthouse Magazine*. "I like to walk away from a sport on top."

//

Having dominated snowboarding so early in the sport's history, Palmer peaked well before the sport's Olympic debut in 1998. As a die-hard patriot

// Saas-Fee, Switzerland, on a Palmer photo shoot in 1994.

with a personal rivalry against "the Euros" though, he couldn't pass up the opportunity to participate in an event that would be the ultimate venue to show what Palmer was made of.

"He went to one of the Grand Prix events to try to qualify [for the 2002 Olympics]," says Bud Fawcett, a representative for Palmer Snowboards, "but he's not up to par on all the spin tricks. He's a great rider in the halfpipe. He's the same old Shaun. But all the technical stuff you need for the Olympics, you gotta train to do that." After riding with one of Palmer U.S.A.'s team members and top halfpipe contender, Andy Finch, Palmer quickly realized how far the halfpipe had come and decided, instead, to focus on motocross.

Though Palmer had faded somewhat from the snowboarding spotlight and had retired from professional mountain biking, ESPN awarded him an ESPY for Action-Sports Athlete of the Year in 2001, a crowning achievement that acknowledged life-long dedication and excellence. That same year, he secured a personal sponsorship from American Honda, which meant that he promoted the brand in everything he did, including the X-Games. In exchange, he received factory support for racing the 250cc National motocross circuit.

Motocross has always presented the greatest challenge for Palmer. He calls it the toughest sport in the world. "You can't fake nothing," he says. A lackluster performance in 2001, though, including a crash on his debut at the 2001 Nationals, led Honda to cease its support. There were no hard feelings. Palmer knows more than anyone that results matter. So, like his foray into mountain biking, Palmer started the 2003 season as a self-supported motocrosser, shelling out $60,000 for three Kawasaki bikes and a box van.

Motocross to Palmer is what baseball was to Michael Jordan. He's battling in the professional ranks because he's a gifted athlete, but it's not the same type of domination he's used to. He has to work at it. And like Jordan, there's a good chance Palmer could make a return to his native sport for one more go-round. In January of 2004, the International Olympic Committee announced that men's and women's boardercross were added as new events for the 2006 Winter Games in Torino, Italy. Palmer tested himself at the 2004 X-Games that same month, finishing a disappointing 19th, and he'll be thirty-seven years old when the 2006 Olympics roll around. With a new level of training and discipline, though, which also means "less beer," who knows? As he's proved in the past, it doesn't pay to bet against Shaun Palmer. **//**

// **OPPOSITE, TOP:** The helicopter as tripod while filming in Norway. // **BOTTOM:** Jamie Lynn launches over snowboarding's paparazzi.

A helicopter hovers precisely above a snowy spire with the snowboarder, big-mountain specialist Jeremy Jones, seated on its skid and the music of Thievery Corporation playing in the background. Positioned for a drop-off, he slips onto the precipice, which is scarcely wide enough for his snowboard. He holds an ice axe in one hand for safety, should the snow give way, and signals thumbs-up to the pilot with the other. The heli lifts away and out of sight. Dropping this impossibly steep, near-vertical line between rocks, he disappears out the bottom of the frame. Cut to Jones carving down a steep, treeless face with slough engulfing him on all sides as he picks a route through a cliff band and then points it straight down the mountain at Mach speed. Yes, Jones is a snowboarding movie star. He is performing for *White Balance*, the 2004 quasi-documentary snowboarding movie from Standard Films.

Jones belongs to an elite class of snowboarders casually referred to as the rock stars. This cadre of top athletes perform year-round for the camera, traveling the globe in search of fresh snow, blue skies, and the ultimate terrain. Together with the filmmakers, they're on a mission to get their part. You see, it's all about the part. Getting a part in a movie, which lasts the length of a song but can take an entire year to capture, pays for everything. It pays for travel, gear, and, most importantly, endorsement salaries.

Like actors or musicians, snowboarding film stars represent different tastes or genres within the sport. Many specialize in one aspect, such as big mountain riding or freestyle, and become famous for that. A gifted few, such as Terje Haakonsen, excel in all arenas. Pro-snowboarding cinema has two Jeremy Joneses, but each is distinguished by their respective expertise. The first Jeremy is a veteran big-mountain rider from Jackson Hole, Wyoming. Following the path blazed by pioneers Tom Burt and Jim Zellers, he transformed a background in racing into a film career by riding maddening terrain with flawless technique, making it look easy. Action-sports film seems to run in his family, since his brothers Steve and Todd own the ski-film company Teton Gravity Research. The younger Jeremy rides for Burton as a freestyle specialist. His parts center on snowboard parks, urban handrails, and big airs—mind-blowing tricks as opposed to steep lines.

This subculture exists mostly below the mainstream radar. The films and many of its stars, such as Noah Salasnek, Jim Rippey, J.P. Walker, and Johan Olofsson, achieve fame amongst the cult fans of snowboarding—mostly kids who idolize them and try as they might to imitate their tricks. Like Craig Kelly in the early 1990s, very few of these riders compete. It's not necessary, nor is there much time for it. It's not their job. If, indeed, they had a job description, it might read something like this: Perform for the camera at the highest level, as per the director's will. Travel to winter locations around the globe, wait patiently for the weather to clear, wait some more as the crew sets up, and always stick your landings.

Snowboarding films have been around almost as long as snowboarding. In France, a series entitled *Apocalypse Snow*, in which evil skiers pursue the snowboarding hero (portrayed by European snowboarding pioneer Regis Roland), single-handedly popularized the sport in Europe. In the U.S., a Lake Tahoe–based production company, Fall Line Films, released *Western Front* and *Snowboarders in Exile* in the late 1980s starring, among others, Damian Sanders and Noah Salasnek. The formats were loose and the soundtracks echoed snowboarding's loud, rebellious attitude. As a result, young skiers from all parts of the country, who couldn't see this type of riding first hand, converted to snowboarding in droves. Skateboarders found themselves a winter sport. As snowboarding rounded a corner into the '90s, two brothers—surfers from San Diego—made the move to Tahoe. Dave Hatchett signed on with Avalanche Snowboards as a pro rider. His younger brother Mike manned the camera. So began the story of Standard Films. **//**

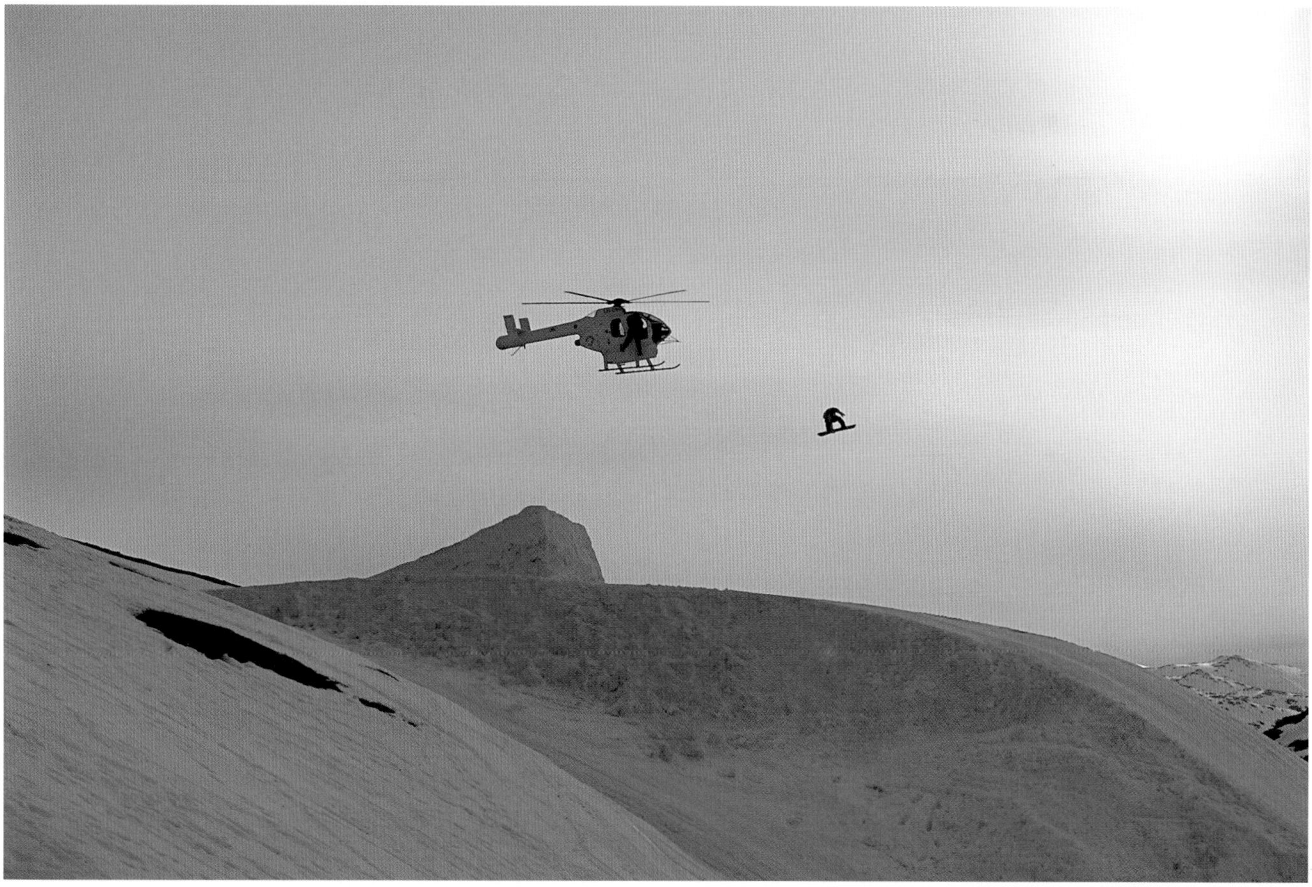

For a select few, snowboarding is the sum total of their career and lifestyle—one that's filled with comedy and drama, conflict and creativity. Over the past decade-and-a-half, Mike Hatchett has captured this unique range of experience and emotion on film. Mixing the clips with carefully chosen soundtracks, he creates snowboarding anthems. Like the iconic 1960s surf film *Endless Summer* and countless others like it, snowboarding films function as windows into the culture of snowboarding, and the sport owes much of its growth and success to the medium. Through these films viewers can connect with the latest personalities, styles, destinations, and tricks, taking virtual journeys around the world of snowboarding, living it, if only for an hour or so. In any given year, the latest snowboard film will offer a state-of-the-union-type address to the fans, indicating where it is at the moment and, more importantly, where it's headed. **//** Using 16-millimeter cameras and a keen sense for action-sports imagery, Tahoe-based filmmaker Mike Hatchett has chronicled the sport's progression from the late 1980s to today. His films translate precipitous riding into passionate viewing, inspiring legions of young snowboarders to take their riding to another level. A documentarian of sorts, Hatchett's work portrays the year-in, year-out exploits of snowboarding's elite riders. In turn, the films help secure sponsorship deals for these individuals who enjoy celebrity status among snowboarding's core audience. For the most part, these riders don't compete, and you won't see them in the Olympics or the X-Games. They're performers with nonstop travel schedules spanning multiple continents and both hemispheres. Such is life for the stars of Standard Films.

// OPPOSITE: Hatchett is lowered on a belay into position somewhere in Alaska, 1996.

//

Standard Films was formed in the early '90s, the brainchild of Mike Hatchett and fellow snowboarding filmmaker, Mike "Mack Dawg" MacEntire. Both were young and ambitious. Both brought experience and resources to the table. "I had more of a big-mountain background, more backcountry," Hatchett says, "and [Mack Dawg] was, like, the freestyle guru. So we decided to make a movie, mixing big mountain and freestyle, and form a company together."

Their first collaboration, *TB2: A New Way of Thinking*, debuted in 1993. According to company literature, the film was a "wake-up call to a whole generation of snowboarders and filmmakers, not to mention the die-hard ski industry, that snowboarding represented the razor-sharp edge of an entirely new era." Though it sounds like hyperbole, the film did exactly that. Integrating performances from Tom Burt, Noah Salasnek, and Dave Hatchett (Mike's brother), it represented big-mountain riding at its most burly and featured some of the first-ever Alaskan heli-snowboarding shots. "There were probably twenty people that were skiing or snowboarding in Valdez," Hatchett recalls. "There were no guides; it was total cowboy." Mack Dawg, on the other hand, fused a different vision of snowboarding: the progressive freestyle onslaught of Terje Haakonsen, Jamie Lynn, and Daniel Franck. "It was a perfect working scenario," Hatchett remembers, "because we were coming from two totally different ends of the spectrum." As the film title suggests though, this wasn't Hatchett's first foray into snowboard films.

The Hatchett brothers grew up in the Solana Beach area of San Diego. "We used to skate Del Mar Skate Ranch back in the day," he says, referring to the iconic 1980s skateboarding hotspot. The two were more-or-less raised on the beach, where learning to surf follows as naturally as learning to ride a bike. Indeed, the board-sports culture was in their blood.

Mike attended the local community college, eventually earning a degree in photography, but somehow the studio didn't feel right. Rock climbing helped him to confirm his instinct. "Dave was a rock climber—big time into climbing," Mike says. "He invited me up to Joshua Tree for a week, and I instantly got hooked. I was still in school at that time, so I started shooting photos of climbing and bringing them back to class and developing them in the dark room. And I started thinking to myself, 'This is cool, I could maybe become a sports photographer.'" By this time, Dave was already a pro snowboarder living in Lake Tahoe. In 1988, however, it seemed to Mike that the scene was congregating in Breckenridge, Colorado, and his first encounters after he committed to checking it out would validate his suspicions.

"When I was driving into [Breckenridge], I saw this kicker that these guys had built in front of their house," Hatchett remembers. "So I grabbed my board and started hitting this jump. These two guys walked out and one of them was Nick Perata and

// **OPPOSITE, TOP:** Hatchett enjoying the perks. // **BOTTOM:** The shooter and his trusty 16mm.

// Valdez, Alaska: The North Shore of snowboarding and a snowboarding cinematographer's dreamscape.

// Mike Hatchett taking viewers along for the ride in 1994.

the other guy was Pat Solomon. And it happened to be that we instantly hit it off. I talked to Nick and he was like, 'Dude, you're a photographer?' Two days later, I met Andy Hetzel and Shawn Farmer."

By the end of the season, Hatchett, Solomon, and Perata found themselves in Tahoe just in time for Squaw Valley to open its slopes to snowboarders for the first time. Solomon had already convinced Hatchett to give filming a shot, and his brother Dave, sponsored by Avalanche at the time, introduced him to Jerry Dugan of Fall Line Films (FLF), a local production company. FLF produced one of the earliest snowboard films, *Western Front*, that season, which included riding from both Mike and Dave. Meanwhile, Solomon and Hatchett prepared to produce, shoot, and edit their own film the following season in 1989.

If *TB2* is Mike Hatchett's *Reservoir Dogs*, then *Totally Board* is *My Best Friend's Birthday* (Quentin Tarantino's obscure directorial debut). The original *TB*, that is, *Totally Board*, was released in 1990, though few had a chance to see it. A quasi-guide to the sport, it followed Dave Hatchett, Nick Perata, and Shaun Farmer from Squaw Valley to Breckenridge, Mount Baker, and Alaska (sans the helicopters), but it lacked significant distribution. What's more, the film came out against Fall Line's second release, *Snowboarders in Exile*, that *International Snowboard* lauded as tapping "the jugular vein of the snowboarding lifestyle/attitude."

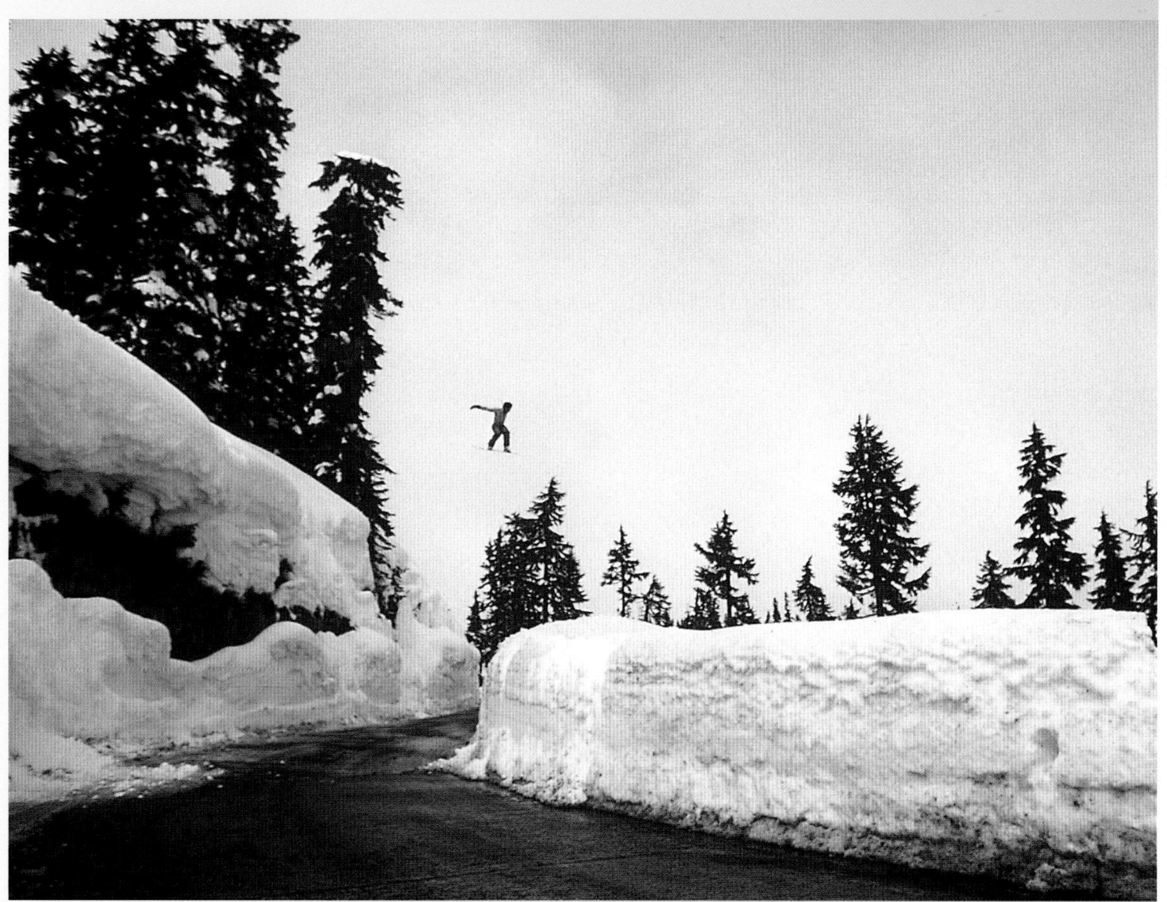

// Shawn Farmer, launching a road-gap jump near Mount Baker in one of the early *TB* films.

Totally Board ultimately lost money. Hatchett chalked it up as a learning experience and proceeded to shoot for FLF on its next two films, the now classic *Critical Condition* and *Riders on the Storm*, before teaming up with Mack Dawg in 1992. Today, *TB* marks a solid chapter in snowboarding history, one that includes Shawn Farmer's groundbreaking road jump near Mount Baker. It also represents the foundation upon which the Standard Films legacy was built.

After making *TB4: Run to the Hills* in the 1995–96 season, Hatchett and MacEntire ended their relationship amicably. "Mack Dawg just decided he wanted to make freestyle-only films," Hatchett says. "He didn't really have an interest in the big-mountain riding. We shook hands and parted ways. It was totally cool." Hatchett credits MacEntire for his professionalism and for letting him keep the Standard Films name. "For that I will be forever grateful," he says. Mack Dawg Productions has since produced influential snowboard films in its own right, capturing the ever-evolving freestyle world.

The Hatchett brothers teamed up once and for all as partners in Standard Films, continuing the *TB* series through its tenth chapter and beyond. In 2003, they were honored with a lifetime achievement award from *Transworld Snowboarding* magazine. Their most recent release, *Lost in Transition*, came out in 2004. The brothers continue to live and work in Lake Tahoe—that is, when they're not traveling the world, filming snowboarding's next superstar. **//**

>LET THE GAMES BEGIN: **ESPN X-GAMES VS. THE OLYMPIC GAMES**

Nineteen ninety-four was a Winter Olympics year and, though snowboarding had not been officially admitted into the Games, a cultural exhibition of the sport was scheduled in Lillehammer, Norway. In a somewhat controversial move, the Federation Ski International (FIS), sanctioning body for international skiing, forced the cancellation of the demonstration. Later that summer, the FIS flouted the International Snowboarding Federation (ISF), snowboarding's governing organization at the time, by voting to include the sport under its own jurisdiction. In other words, snowboarding would become an Olympic sport. It would debut at Nagano, Japan, in 1998, with both halfpipe and alpine disciplines, but it would be sanctioned and organized under the auspices of a skiing organization. For all intents and purposes, in the eyes of the International Olympic Committee (IOC), snowboarding was (and remains) just one of many ski disciplines. For a sport that had rebelled against the mainstream skiing establishment, this did not sit well with those who'd dedicated their lives to building it to be distinct.

Meanwhile, in spring of the same year, the cable network ESPN held a press conference at Planet Hollywood in New York City announcing that the first Extreme Games—a festival of action sports, loud music, and corporate sponsors—would be held the following year.

Fast forward to the winter of 1996—ESPN's event was now called the X-Games, and the first winterized version, with snowboarding topping the list of sports, debuted in Big Bear Lake, California. The event was televised to 198 countries and territories in twenty-one different languages.

In ten short years, snowboarding has become the anchor for the Winter X-Games, with seven different events such as slopestyle and big air. There is no place for alpine racing—it just doesn't mesh with the pace and visual power of the X-Games. In this way, the X-Games reflect snowboarding's connection to skateboarding, complete with heavy doses of attitude and individuality. In contrast, the Olympics see snowboarding as an offshoot of skiing and treat it as a team sport with uniforms and coaches. While a gold medal in an Olympic event is undeniably representative of high-level achievement and ability, and brings with it as much or more international recognition as an X-Games win, many riders believe the X-Games are truer to what the sport of snowboarding really is.

Still, the X-Games and the Olympics have managed to find common ground in two riders—two ambassadors for the sport—who, in some ways, represent opposite ends of the snowboarding spectrum.

Ross Powers grew up in Vermont and started snowboarding when he was eight years old in rather unforgiving Northeast conditions. Pegged as a prodigy, he received a scholarship to the prestigious Stratton Mountain School in Stratton, Vermont, an institution renowned for grooming World Cup skiers. Powers competed in his first U.S. Open with his fourth-grade classmates in audience, and he's since won the title twice. Where many in the sport have tattoos, Powers has pedigree. He's the consummate professional and a nice guy in general—two characteristic Olympic qualities. His approach to halfpipe competition is methodical and almost single-minded, which is more commonplace in skiing but quite rare in the raucous world of snowboarding.

Described as one of the most technically progressive pipe riders in the world, Danny Kass grew up in middle-class New Jersey. While Powers competed in the U.S. Open, Kass, who is a few years younger, rode backyard skateboard ramps with his older brother Matt. The two got into snowboarding at local New Jersey ski areas, and Danny even ventured north to Vermont for a couple seasons. But joining his brother in Mammoth Lakes, California, would truly set the stage for his riding. A hotbed for freestyle with a dominant SoCal influence, Kass rounded out his riding repertoire and took it to another level. With a wiseass

// The rebel champion, Danny Kass, picking up his first of two U.S. Open halfpipe titles in 2002, only a month after winning the Olympic silver medal in the same event in Park City, Utah.

PHILIPS
PHILIPS US OPEN SNOWBOARDING CHAMPIONSHIPS
PHILIPS
BURTON SNOWBOARDS
STRATTON
BURTON SNOWBOARDS
PHILIPS
PHILIPS
Jeep
RIGHT RIGHT

// **OPPOSITE:** Wherever he goes, Ross Powers sets the high bar on amplitude. It is what made the difference between gold and silver in the 2002 Olympic halfpipe event.

reputation and ultra-hip image (he popularized wearing DJ-style headphones while riding), Kass defines what an X-Games competitor ought to be. He competes at the highest level in all freestyle events, goes huge, plays to the fans, and comes across as a rebel.

Powers and Kass found themselves on the 2002 U.S. Olympic Snowboard Freestyle team, along with teammate Tommy Czeschin. As fate would have it, the X-Games began January 17 in Aspen, Colorado—where snowboarding was only first permitted months prior—and would be broadcast February 1–5 on ESPN and ABC. Opening ceremonies in Salt Lake, some 350 miles away, commenced February 8.

As reigning X-Games SuperPipe champion, Kass showed up to defend his title against the likes of his teammates and other major contenders including Keir Dillon, Shaun White, and J.J. Thomas, who was on the fence for selection to the Olympic team. In front of 35,000 spectators, J.J. Thomas snatched the gold, which put him on the fast track to Salt Lake with Kass, Powers, and Czeschin.

By the 2002 Olympics, the halfpipe of snowboarding's Olympic debut in 1998 had grown into the superpipe—an exaggerated version of the original with seventeen-foot walls, which is now the international standard for competition. Both Mammoth and Stratton are premier superpipe venues, so Kass and Powers felt right at home on the Park City turf. Powers entered Salt Lake with a bronze medal from Nagano in 1998, so he already had "world stage" experience. On the women's team, Shannon Dunn brought a bronze from Nagano with her to Park City as well, and young Kelly Clark had just come off a gold-medal finish at the X-Games.

A crowd of 25,000 people showed up for the men's and women's halfpipe finals in Park City. A survey by Leisure Trends later found that thirty-two percent of the total U.S. population (92 million people) tuned in to watch the event. It's safe to say snowboarding owned the spotlight. Kelly Clark was the first to fully revel in it, winning the first Olympic gold medal in U.S. snowboarding history. On her heels, Ross Powers, Danny Kass, and J.J. Thomas swept the men's final—gold, silver, and bronze, respectively—making history once again as the first U.S. Winter Olympic medal sweep since 1956.

Unlike a number of other events, such as ski jumping or luge, the Olympics don't own snowboarding. At most, the Olympics represent a small fraction of the sport's much greater whole. The IOC may not recognize snowboarding as a sport independent of skiing, but as of 2002 it quickly learned that snowboarding—in particular, the superpipe event—spoke to the new generation, something ESPN has known all along. This is perhaps why riders have more respect for the X-Games, why they feel it's more "core" and true to the sport of snowboarding. After all, skiing wasn't represented, nor was it necessary, at the first Winter X-Games. In 2002, organizers added Ski Slopestyle and Ski SuperPipe events. How ironic will it be when the IOC recognizes these as skiing disciplines? Might skiing then become an aspect of snowboarding? **//**

Like a top supermodel or the artist currently known as Prince, the greatest snowboarder in the world is recognized by first name alone. Mentioning this name triggers an array of superlatives: he goes the biggest, wins the most, rides the fastest, and just does everything the best. When it comes to riding a snowboard, he's practically infallible. And with all that's been written about him, he's secured mythic status as both athlete and Norwegian. This is what it means to be Terje. // The five-time world champion meets me in the lobby of a hotel in Stratton, Vermont, where he has shown up unannounced to the U.S. Open, and he's right on time. Notorious for marching to the beat of his own drum, which includes avoiding journalists, such punctuality for an interview that would undoubtedly focus on him was hardly to be expected. Terje is modest and soft spoken for a rider of such monumental prowess—he has very few words for the press and even fewer about himself. The five-foot-nine legend shuffles through the lobby dressed in sweats and slippers, and we retreat to a far corner of the adjacent restaurant, where some fellow pros are preparing for the day's superpipe competition. Outside it snows heavily. The flakes fall on a near-vertical path with extreme grace—not unlike Terje landing his huge airs. Part of what has bolstered Terje to living-legend status is the unique, give-and-take relationship he's established with gravity—it's as if the two forces spar with the mutual respect of master swordsmen. It is a magnificent thing to witness. // In 2004, Haakonsen turned thirty. Exactly half his life has been devoted to professional snowboarding. And in many ways, it all started when the would-be phenomenon showed up here, at the U.S. Open, at age fifteen. Two of his idols, Craig Kelly

// **OPPOSITE:** Terje Haakonse as ambassador, organizer, and competitor at his own Arctic Challenge Big Air event in 200

and Jeff Brushie, were competing, yet he wowed fellow competitors and the audience alike with his skill. Like seeing Tiger Woods at his first Masters or Michael Jordan in his first NBA finals, most knew they'd witnessed something exceptional. Indeed, it seems Terje's status in the world of snowboarding cannot be overstated. "There is a deeper fire born of small-town Scandinavia, a wintry pride, along with a streak of Hessianism which drives [Terje] to do the thing at hand a bit gnarlier every time," wrote *Frequency* editor Jeff Galbraith. Looking at the bigger picture—the one that includes ancestry—this fiery Scandinavian pride appears to have deeper origins. To find them, one need only to explore Terje's heritage: a tradition rooted in both Norway and its national pastime.

//

Born on October 11, 1974, Terje Haakonsen grew up in the Telemark region of southern Norway in the village of Romot. His father worked as a chef and his mother taught special education, and they weren't especially athletic. With an older brother and younger sister, the family lived comfortably but had little left over for luxuries such as tropical vacations or snowboarding gear. Terje learned skiing as an early rite of passage: cross-country at age three and alpine when he was five. Terje and his brother built ski jumps in their backyard, and riding plastic miniskis, he caught air for the first time and in no time mastered 360s.

Tapping a birthright of sorts, young Haakonsen was following in the footsteps of his ancestors. The Norwegian identity is derived as much from its ancient myths and legends as it is from the sport of skiing. Symbolizing freedom and triumph, skiing is a source of national pride. In building a ski jump in his back yard, Terje unknowingly paid homage to Sondre Norheim, a fellow resident of Telemark who is universally acknowledged as the father of modern skiing.

Norheim's status in Norway is like that of America's Thomas Jefferson and Babe Ruth rolled into one. A poor cotter and gifted craftsman from the town of Morgedal, he pioneered all aspects of the sport in the late 1800s from bindings and sidecut to methods and disciplines. The undisputed master of the slopes, his inventions and techniques lead to the first freestyle contests. Like Terje today, he was known for his daring and skill in the air.

Norheim immigrated to the United States in 1884, where he resigned to cross-country skiing in the flatlands of North Dakota. The countrymen he left behind in the nation that had been under Swedish rule since 1814 meanwhile sought a means to gaining their independence. They found it through skiing and a man named Fridtjof Nansen.

In 1888, Nansen became the first man to cross the mid-Greenland ice cap—on skis, of course. "In a country with no embassies and no diplomacy," wrote Odd Molster in *Skiing and the Creation of a Norwegian Identity*, "a skiing hero became the first Norwegian conqueror since the Vikings, the first

// **OPPOSITE:** Haakonsen is just as comfortable in midair as the rest of us are in a La-Z-Boy. // **FOLLOWING SPREAD:** Soaring above the halfpipe at The Arctic Challenge in 2000. // Toying with gravity above a quarterpipe hit in Switzerland, 2001.

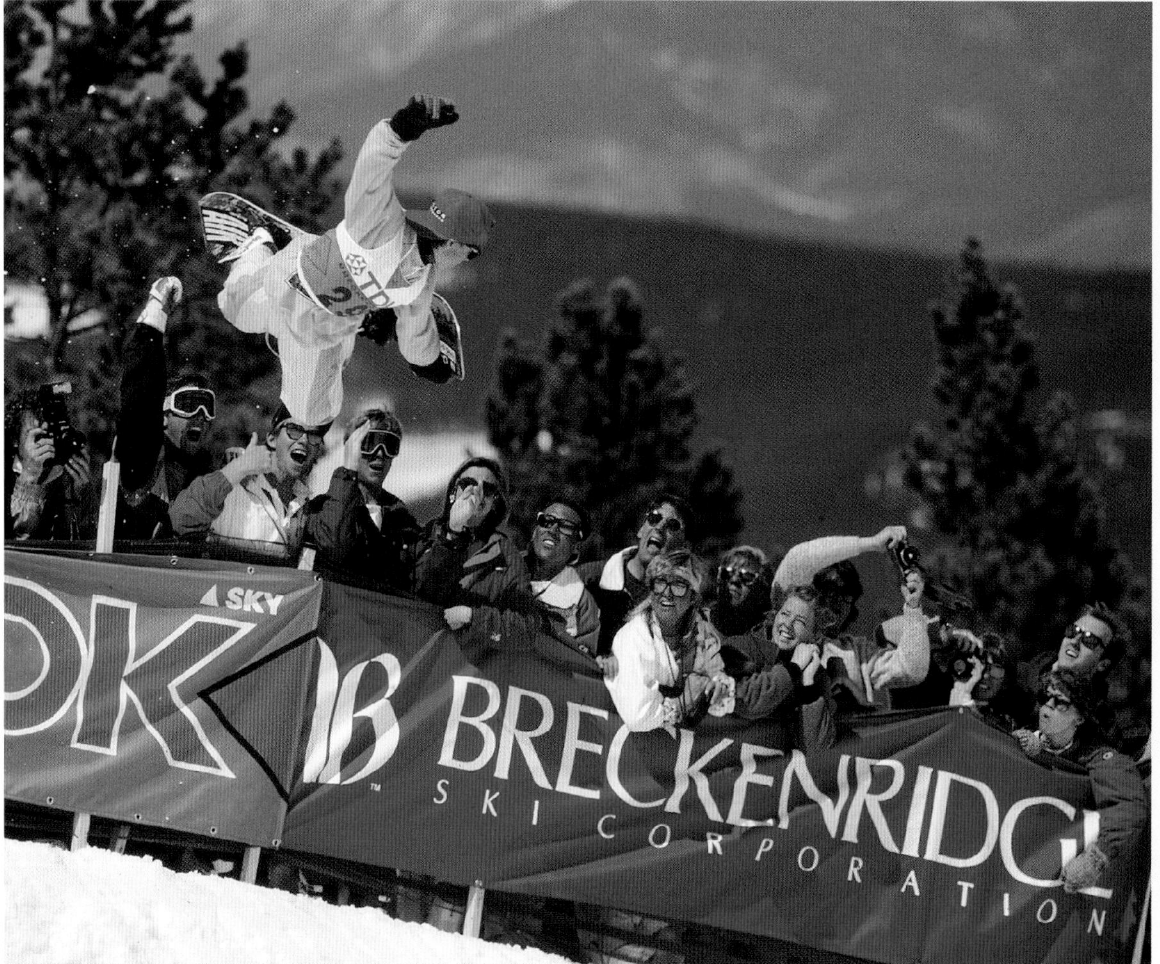

// Allow me to introduce myself: Terje makes his debut at the 1990 World Championships in Breckenridge, Colorado.

true Norwegian abroad in eight hundred years." The famous explorer later made a valiant attempt at crossing the North Pole on skis in 1895. Despite failing, he nevertheless inspired a nation. Norway secured its independence shortly thereafter in 1905, and a year later, it crowned King Haakon VII, the seventh in a line of Norwegian kings that share Terje's surname, and entered a new era.

//

In the Telemark region in the winter of 1987—eighty-two years since Haakon VII assumed the throne of a liberated Norway in the same place where Sondre Norheim gave birth to modern-day skiing—Terje Haakonsen made his first snowboard turns.

"I remember at first, I was like, 'This is really hard,'" he says, describing his first attempts. "My feet would fall out of the bindings because I was twelve and I was small for my age. And then I remember trying it in powder, where you don't really need all that support. I was really hooked after I tried it in powder."

Inside of three years, Terje mastered snowboarding, signed a sponsorship deal with Burton, and began competing at the highest level. Inspired by teammates Craig Kelly and Jeff Brushie, Terje learned from the masters. "I *was* Craig Kelly," he admits, "in everything—style, tricks, everything."

The proverbial torch was being passed. Kelly, the first "greatest snowboarder ever," was bridging from competition to pure freeriding just as Terje came into his own. Kelly would later acknowledge his good timing. In 1992, Terje beat Shaun Palmer to win his first of three U.S. Open halfpipe titles. Conveniently, Kelly didn't hang around long enough to get beat.

As Norheim did for skiing, Haakonsen took the young sport of snowboarding and revolutionized nearly every aspect of it. He dominated most competitive disciplines from halfpipe and big air to the Mount Baker Legendary Banked Slalom. Like Kelly and Palmer before him, Terje honed his racing skills in addition to freestyle. After all, the term "slalom" originated in Norway with Norheim himself. So it comes as no surprise—call it a genetic predisposition—that he's won the Banked Slalom six times (and counting). What gave Haakon the Great mythic status, though, was his performance at Mount Baker in 1998, when he dropped into the course fakie (yes, backwards) and still finished in fourth in the qualifying round. Of course, the next day he won the event. As Terje humbled the field in Washington, snowboarding prepared to make its Olympic debut in Nagano, Japan. Of Terje's many conquests throughout the world of snowboarding, there's one for which he'll always be known, for better or worse. The world's best rider respectfully declined to compete in—or

// Brian Iguchi, John Cardiel, and Haakonsen in the back seat of filmmaker Dave Seoane's Cadillac during a roadtrip for the film *Roadkill*.

// **OPPOSITE:** Haakonsen took home the $20,000 first-prize purse from this 2003 Big Air event in Japan.

to even acknowledge—the Olympics. But it wasn't a boycott.

"That was just made up by the press," he says, discounting the sensational headlines. "I was just like, 'I'm not going to join that party,' you know? There are just so many elements about how they run things I really was not stoked on."

Likening the International Olympic Committee (IOC) to the mafia and its chairman to Al Capone, Haakon the Convicted stirred up quite the controversy. "When I say 'mafia,' I mean what most people see in the word: people who take over control but never let anyone have an inside look at what they are doing," Haakonsen told a Swedish news channel. As a result, he single-handedly called into question the validity of a gold medal. "Every snowboarder who came to the Olympics basically knew he was battling it out for second," said fellow pro snowboarder Peter Line. And then there's the politics. "How can you have a sponsor for ten years," he asked rhetorically, "and then you go to the Olympics and you can't even pack your own bags because the nation has sold you as a package?"

Ironically enough, considering his heritage, Terje harbors very little nationalistic pride. "Norway is a really great country to live," he says, "but it's never supported me like my sponsors. My flag should be Burton not Norway." Mostly, though, he takes it personally when the Olympics, or anyone else for that matter, portray the sport in a less-than-ideal light. "If snowboarding isn't delivered on a high level and very professionally, it looks like kids are just playing," he says. "[The riders] should decide how we want to look out there."

In 2000, Haakonsen backed up such convictions and criticisms by co-founding the Arctic Challenge, a yearly event held on his home turf that invites only the best twenty-some riders in the world to compete. He listens to riders' wants and tailors the competition accordingly in an attempt to create an event that generates respect for the sport rather than profiteers from it. In the inaugural year of the Arctic challenge, Terje won both the quarterpipe and halfpipe. These days, despite participating in only a handful of international competitions, he's still consistently on the podium. "I normally do, like, five," each season he says. He's not the dominant force of, say, four years ago. Did he expect to win at the U.S. Open where we met? "No," he says, fairly certain that that's out of the question. "I've had two days in the pipe this year, and I have a sore back." Indeed, he wouldn't even qualify for the finals. Not to mention, rehab kept him from shooting with Standard Films that season, something he's done every year since the early 1990s.

//

Terje is a master of all trades, from World Cup halfpipes to death-defying Alaskan lines. He's got the vision to push innovation and the physical and technical ability to pull it off. "He's the kind of kid who is afraid of nothing," says Jake Burton. So, like everything else he undertakes, Haakon the Brave took freeriding to another level.

// Terje contemplating the line.

// Air . . . apparent. //
OPPOSITE: Terje fusing freestyle and big-mountain riding in Whistler Blackcomb, 2002.

The teenage king changed the face of big-mountain riding, and chocked up another triumphant conquest. "He was one of the first to mix freestyle with big-mountain riding," says Mike Hatchett, "to, you know, spin a 360 into a line and slash a wave and spin another three. In *TB4*, he does a big frontside 180 off a cliff—a solid forty-foot cliff—and lands it. That's typical Terje. He's just the master."

Haakon the Dad now has two children, both boys, with his long-time girlfriend. He lives in Oslo when he's home but spends a lot of time in Asia, South America, Hawaii, and Southern California. It's safe to say that Terje, considering the physical and psychological demands of professional snowboarding, has crossed into the autumn of his career and the twilight of his reign. Having amassed a small fortune and made history, he has also accumulated his fair share of injuries, and there are visible chinks in his armor. But there is also nothing left for him to prove—nothing in the world of snowboarding, that is. In 2004, he qualified for Norway's Bygodoey soccer team (third division) as a right wing, so the saga of Haakon the Athlete is ongoing. Only history will have complete perspective on his impact as both an athlete and national hero. **//**

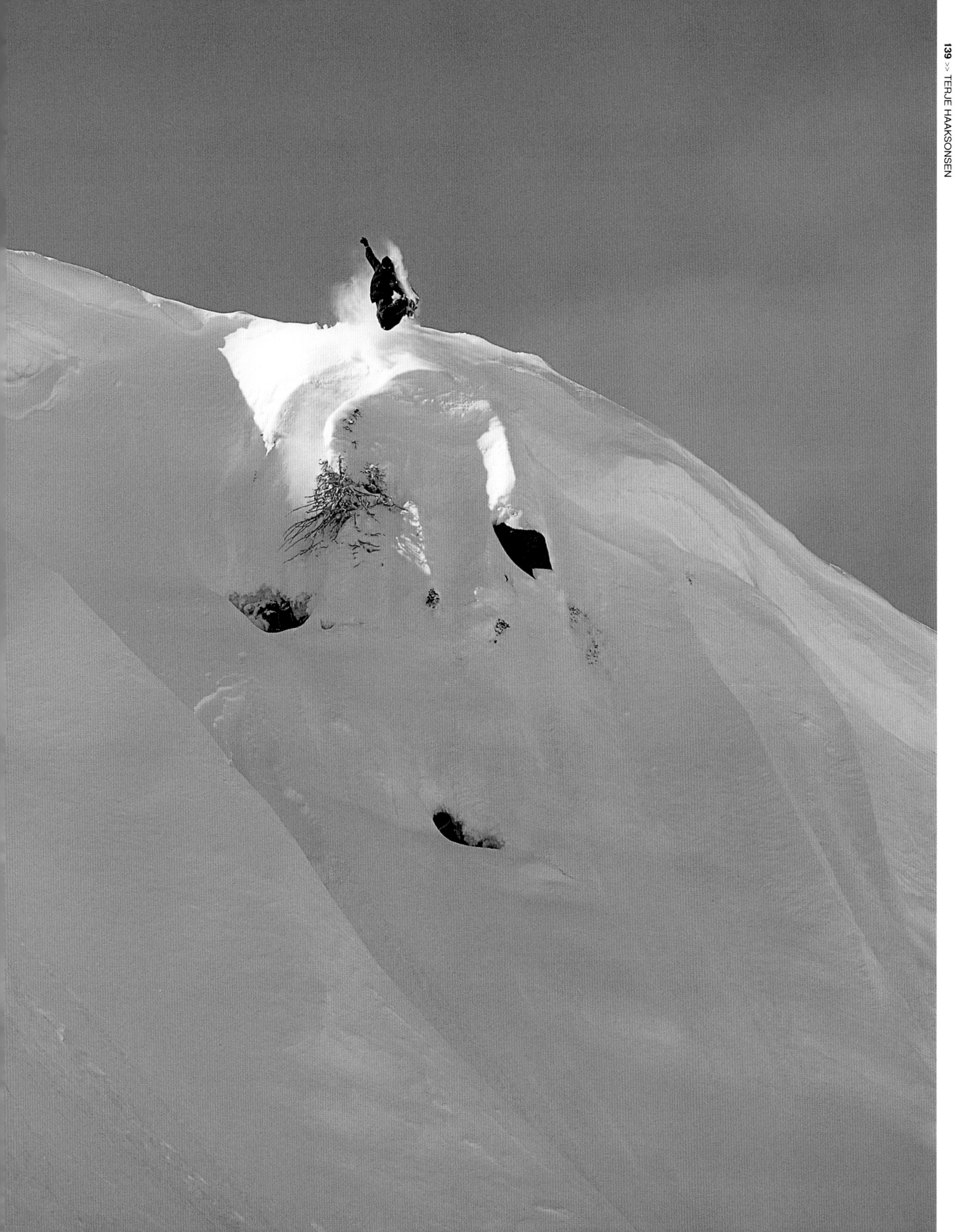

>THE COUP: **NEW-SCHOOL SNOWBOARDING**

Summit County, Colorado, became a hotbed of progressive, hardcore snowboarding in 1986 when the World Championships moved to Breckenridge. Nearby towns such as Dillon and Leadville offered affordable living for the dedicated who flocked to the new winter Mecca in droves. Other resorts in the region, such as Copper Mountain and Arapahoe Basin, embraced the young sport earlier than others. The snowboarding media scoured Summit County in search of new talent, and it found not only talent but a new way of riding—a new form of expression. The style was aggressive, creative, and deemed skiers the enemy. Needless to say, it was chock-full of attitude.

// ABOVE: A pioneer of the new school movement, Andy Hetzel rail slides this log just as the term "jib" entered snowboarding vocabulary, c. 1989. **// OPPOSITE:** Rider Mike Basich takes street-style skateboarding, complete with graffiti and picnic tables, to the snow in 1991.

Around the same time, skateboarding experienced a major shift in style from flamboyant vert riding to a more aggressive form known as street skating. Almost overnight, the ramp lords of the time, international superstars such as Christian Hosoi, Steve Caballero, and Mike McGill, faded from the spotlight. The demise of '80s vert skating is chronicled in the documentary *Stoked*, a 2003 film by Helen Stickler about the rise and fall of skateboarding pop star Mark "Gator" Rogowski, whose career crumbled tragically in the wake of street skating and then ended abruptly with a murder conviction. His style and signature-model skateboard by Vision were icons. Vision also owned the license for Sims Snowboards at the time, and as flashy vert riding went the way of hair metal, the company filed for bankruptcy. Grunge music, spawning out of the Northwest, swept the nation, and along with it came a major shift in attitude and fashion, particularly among Generation X. In this fervent atmosphere of innovation, the new school was called into session.

"Earth tones, oversized street clothes, and beanie hats replaced neon, ski clothes, and headbands. Flatland spinning tricks and rail slides replaced lofty aerials. Behavior became increasingly outrageous. In the most intense period of skier–snowboarder conflict, the media churned out sensationalized reports of having gang wars on the hills—snowboarders carrying guns, dealing drugs, and threatening innocent skiers," writes Susanna Howe in *Sick: A Cultural History of Snowboarding*. Snowboarders became increasingly fractionalized. The hardcore riders vibed the influx of new riders who, in their opinion, latched onto the sport like a fashion trend. More so, they resented skiers, whose elitism conspired to ban snowboarding at many resorts and who just weren't cool. Howe continues, "Much as skateboarding and surfing ended their association in the late '70s, snowboarding

// **OPPOSITE:** Whatever this thing is, it just got jibbed. // **ABOVE:** Why take the stairs when you can ride the railing?

// **OPPOSITE:** Huge backside 360s, like this one by Jamie Lynn, are what inspired others like Peter Line to add more revolutions and corkscrew spins. The incredible number of variations on this theme required an entire language of new trick terms.

separated from skiing and took on the increasingly urban, aggressive attitude of skateboarding in the early '90s."

This ultimately meant a new bag of tricks and self-expression. Snowboarders started "jibbing," a creative and potentially destructive type of riding where one incorporates both natural and manmade obstacles into the downhill flow. It started, more or less, by riding fallen trees on the mountain and progressed to pedestrian handrails near the base area—anything in their path that could somehow be ridden. This called for changes in equipment. Boards needed to be shorter and stances needed to be wider in order to perform. Many took to modifying their boards by sawing off the tips and tails and drilling different sets of holes for the bindings. Putting as much distance as possible between themselves and skiers, the new-schoolers eschewed high-tech ski clothing for the less-functional baggy jeans and thick flannels made popular by the grunge movement.

With much help from the media, including a new magazine named *Blunt*, which answered the new-school calling, this zeitgeist of sorts spread to every corner of snowboarding's domain. Companies responded with new boards and a fresh take on snowboard attire. Resorts responded to the desires of this vastly expanding market of young boarders and equipped parks with handrails, picnic tables, and even cars in some cases—all for the express purpose of jibbing.

Higher on the mountain and in the backcountry, others were building massive jumps called kickers. Also known as the "cheese wedge" for their large, triangular shape, these grew in size and so elevated the ceiling of possibility. This period saw a significant drop in competitive participation since it was seen as too institutionalized—too much like skiing. Instead, the snowboard video dominated as the medium of choice for performing, getting sponsored, and pushing the sport to new levels. Eventually, the new-school style of riding spawned its own competitive events; the culmination of park riding became the slopestyle event, and getting big air became, well, big air. Two of the most influential riders to explode from the new-school movement and achieve a modicum of international fame were Peter Line and Tara Dakides. **//**

Peter Line finds inspiration where others find the urge to flush. *Beautiful Nubian Princess* and *The Misfits* are two works by this part-time artist and career snowboarding mastermind. Unveiled in the pages of *Snowboarder Magazine* in late 2001, the works reflected his out-of-the-box approach, the same *modus operandi* he's used to shape the sport of snowboarding for more than a decade. They give a sense of Peter Line's need to express himself and show his ability to see things in a different light. In these creations, Line photographed a series of urine samples—his own, still fresh in the bowl—and then animated the porcelain-framed images with a black magic marker, bringing life to otherwise meaningless excrement. // This brand of juvenile toilet humor, though somewhat crass, appeals to a certain demographic—the actual teenagers who turn to *Snowboarder* for entertainment and access to snowboarding's superstars. Line knows the readers find it funny because he knows what it's like to be in their shoes—or boots, as the case may be. He's true to himself and true to snowboarding and true to the kids who idolize him. Peter Line is true to the core. // The Washington native is perhaps the greatest visionary in snowboarding's modern era, innovating everything from trickery to technical clothing and, yes, art. With abundant creativity comes a certain level of eccentricity. He's outside the ordinary, at least by some standards. Working as a commentator for ESPN at the 2001 X-Games when he couldn't compete because of a broken arm, Line's on-camera work was deemed "too weird" by the network's head honchos. As for the kids, his nonconformist—at times outrageous—style is indicative of being "core." In his opinion, it's "the way

// OPPOSITE: The man ESPN deemed too controversial to comment on camera for the X-Games.

A song originally wri
ten acoustically right
after the band was
signed to Geffen Records,
only to be transformed in
rehearsal, and live, into the
version heard on Appetite
AN SUES EX-WIFE,
he took my sperm
thout permission"
CAN AXL HELP YOU?
IF YOU'VE got a problem, I'm here to
Please write Conspiracy, Inc., P.O. Box
Los Angeles, CA 9006? You must enclose a
self-addressed envelope for a confidential
reply or one of my leaflets.
To Love Her
Crazy
n A Million
VICAR

snowboarding should be," as opposed to going mainstream, which necessarily follows from national television coverage and what many contend is exploitation of the sport.

To the extent that snowboarding is an industry, to the degree that it's a cultural movement and a form of self-expression, Peter Line is a leader. He's an entrepreneur and an artist. He does it all. "His riding, his companies, his movies, any interview," says photographer Jeff Curtes, "anything the guy touches turns into something hugely influential."

Line turned pro and made snowboarding his career and his life's work. Now into his thirties, he can't push the envelope the way he used to after fifteen years of riding hard. "I'm feeling the pain a little bit in the joints," he says when I interview the aging icon from his home near Seattle, Washington. But that's not all. He's also backing away from the sport because "the motivation level is dropping." An almost pathological innovator with a keen sense for developing an image and the importance of how your image is perceived, Peter Line thrives on creating and mastering new tricks. Furthermore, he's inspired to stoke young snowboarders and shudders at the prospect of letting them down. The problem, besides aching joints, is that he's innovated himself (and the sport) into a corner. "When I started, snowboarding was relatively new. There was still a lot to learn and work on," he says. In other words, when Peter Line got into it, snowboarding's toilet bowl was still a fresh canvas.

//

Born August 3, 1974, in Media, Pennsylvania, Peter Line grew up in Bellevue, Washington. He discovered skateboarding as a young teenager when the sport was booming nationwide. In middle and high schools throughout the country, groups of skaters rebelled against team-sports conformity and chose punk rock over pop. *Thrasher* was *the* skateboard magazine, chronicling the latest maneuvers and biggest names. Though it was an individual sport, skate companies organized hand-picked teams of top riders to represent their brand and set forth an image. They produced home videos to stoke and inspire young fans, like Peter Line.

Having already tried skiing—his junior high offered a ski-school program—it was obvious to the thirteen-year-old skater in 1987 that snowboarding was the way to go. "In *Thrasher Magazine* there'd always be a couple pages of snowboarding," he remembers, "and in Washington there wasn't a whole lot of skating you could do in the winter." His parents bought him a Burton Elite 140 for Christmas that year. "It was blue with a swallow tail and a fin," he says. "I remember taking the tail off, but the board still sucked." So much that it stalled his early progression. "I remember not being as good as my friends and always being the last to get to the bottom." The next year, he worked extra chores around the house and sold his old board to buy a Sims Pocketknife 1425. "The year after I got that board, and after having more fun and catching up to my friends, I started falling in love with it more."

// OPPOSITE: Riding a Division 23 board in 1996, Line jibs a wooden post covered in PVC pipe.

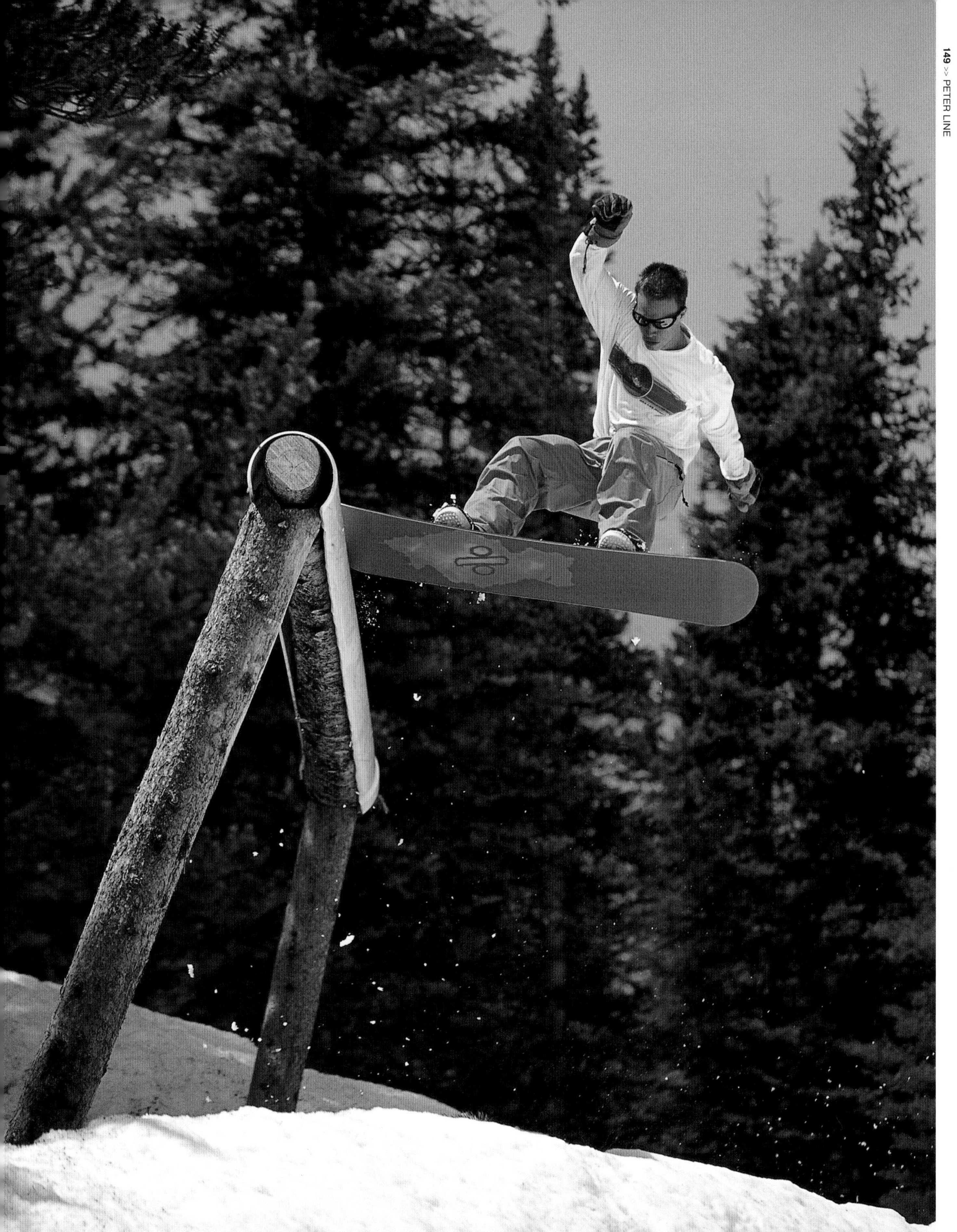

// OPPOSITE: Leading by example—and with his shoulder—Line spins on multiple axes above this quarterpipe hit in 1996.

In 1988, the first-ever snowboarding videos found their way into the VCRs of young hopefuls like Peter Line and his friends. For such a new and progressive sport, videos gave kids everywhere an opportunity to see what the pros—the mythic heroes—were up to and what new tricks they were pulling off in fantasy locations like Tahoe, Vail, and Mount Baker. Only for Line, Baker was practically a local mountain, and the pros were very real people.

"Since Baker was one of the first mountains to allow snowboarding," he says, "there were a lot of good guys who came out of there like Jamie Lynn and Mike Ranquet and the dudes that hung around with them. So we got the chance to actually see good riders in person. Most people only got to see whatever was in the magazines or films, but for us to actually have amazing riders that we'd sometimes see at our own mountains showed us where it can go. Our progression was a lot quicker, I believe, because of that."

Mike Ranquet, a young member of Mount Baker Hard Core (MBHC) and a disciple of Craig Kelly, was sponsored by Sims at the time and doubled as a professional skateboarder. Appearing in a 1988 snowboard video by Sims called *Snow Shredders*, he inspired Line with his progressive style. "People where doing straight airs and rocket airs while he was doing the switch stuff and spinning. He was on the forefront of skate-style snowboarding. And because he was a Northwest guy, he was one of my major influences." Line took a few runs with Ranquet and Kelly the following season at a local ski area called Alpental. "I saw Craig do a J-tear," he remembers. "I was stoked."

Like others before him, Line faced a crossroads after graduating high school in 1993. He'd already placed third at the junior national halfpipe competition in Stratton, Vermont. He'd done summer camp at Mount Hood—a prime scouting venue and where he first connected with top snowboard filmmakers from Mack Dawg Productions—and secured a low-level sponsorship in Division 23. "I somehow convinced my parents to let me take a year off to work and snowboard and see what happened," he recalls. "That year turned into a decade."

//

Growing up in one of snowboarding's soul centers offered Line a head start on others his age. He couldn't help but absorb the MBHC heritage, but he also identified with the kids who were just getting into snowboarding, in the great boom of the mid-1990s. "In that 1993–94 era, snowboarding started to get an image over being just a sport. You were a snowboarder," he insists. "You didn't just snowboard."

Line was among those who drilled into their boards and installed bolts so that they could achieve a wider stance more conducive to doing tricks and riding switch. His mission was not to become world champion or to explore distant mountains by helicopter. "I wanted to learn the newest trick," he says, "to learn them and progress

// The rare shot of Line riding a halfpipe in 1996.

from there and try the next hardest trick and land it a few times and try the next hardest trick." In contests, judges usually value consistency over innovation, and when you're constantly pushing the envelope trying new and different things, it's tough to earn medals. "I would always just go for it," he remembers. "Win or lose, I'm either gonna fall or land doing the biggest trick." This go-for-broke approach didn't win titles, but it looked great on film, and it quickly became his main marketing medium. "My sponsors knew that the marketing was in videos not contests," he says. "At the time, Division 23 was a smaller, core company whereas Burton was a contest-driven company . . . more mainstream."

Line studied snowboard videos to a degree that bordered on obsession. "I'd watch them to the end, rewinding shots, pause tricks in mid-air, then rewind to the beginning and watch it again," he says. "So that's kind of like my whole idea of what professional snowboarding is." But by 1995 Peter was no longer idolizing snowboarding-video stars, he was one.

He got breakthrough parts in both *TB3* and *TB4* by employing a range of trick variations that set him apart. "He started taking kickers to the next level," remembers Mike Hatchett. "When everyone was spinning flat, he started doing more rotations and had really good style—real skate-influenced style, all balled up and not flapping."

Line also ventured into the backcountry but it wasn't to ride untracked powder or to reconnect with Nature. He went to build massive kicker-style jumps, ones big enough for him to pull off the tricks he'd landed in his mind countless times. "He brought the backcountry kicker to the next level," Hatchett continues. "We built a few jumps in the backcountry and filmed them, but [Peter] would stop and take three hours to pile up snow above a transition."

When the kickers were built and the cameras rolled, Line let it rip in a way no one had seen before. "He added new rotations and technical tricks," Hatchett remembers. "He kind of opened up people's minds and said, 'Don't just spin flat,' or 'Don't just do a backside 540; how about a switch backside 540? How about a rodeo this or how about that?' I think he showed people that there was a whole new book of tricks that were going to get invented, and it was just getting started."

Line initiated nothing short of a revolution with his reverse (switch) tricks and corkscrew-style airs. Mack Dawg caught it all on film, so the kids *and* his peers could study and learn them. By then, competitions had evolved to include the Big Air event. Perfectly suited to Line's go-big-or-go-home attitude, the event offered a broader venue in which to showcase his latest trickery. "When the Big Air thing came along, it was the same thing as filming," he says, "just one big jump. And that worked out for me." Line won his first Big Air—his first-ever contest win—at the U.S. Open in 1996 and followed that up a year later with wins at the MTV Sports and Music Festival and Summer X-Games.

// OPPOSITE: Maybe Line's air-time technique didn't come from snowboard videos after all.

f a l c o

// This graphic is from the Division series Peter designs personally for Forum each season. Times may come and go, but Line's individual style has survived the test of time.

//

Snowboarders starting companies was nothing new in 1996. There were the originals, like Burton and Sims, and champions like Bert LaMar, Rob Morrow, and Shaun Palmer parlaying their winning careers into marketable snowboarding brands. Peter Line's foray into this aspect of the snowboarding industry was, as with most everything else he did, different. Instead of waiting until his fame peaked (or waned) to broaden his range, he partnered up and launched a new brand in the thick of his rapidly evolving career.

In 1995, Peter Line and Ingemar Backman, another up-and-comer at the time, launched Four-square Outerwear to answer the needs of young snowboarders. Line's involvement wasn't just endorsement: "I designed all the clothing for the first six years," he says. "When it first started, my designs were very tech for more extreme weather, since I was coming from Washington." His sense of style translated from tricks to clothing; functional aspects and fashion appeal were equally important, and Line's stamp of approval carried supreme value. It was cool because it had to be. "Anything with my name on it, I wanted to be completely perfect," he says. "I didn't want somebody designing it so-so and putting it in the market and having the kids go, 'Peter's clothes suck.'" He remembered from his days as a "kid" how their brutal scrutiny could make or break a rider, along with whatever brand he endorsed. In the game of pro snowboarding, your image is your currency, and a shitty image will lead to bankruptcy.

Line had a signature snowboard model from his first board sponsor, Division 23, starting in 1994, and a year later it was selling well. "I had just started to become the biggest-name rider out there as far as marketing goes," he says. "I was kind of the new kid on the block, so everybody was watching me." But

// LEFT TO RIGHT: Peter Line's pro-model for Division 2006, and yet another example of his graphic style. // Two boards from Forum's Destroyer series, which have long been recognized as the boards of choice for riders on their way to pro models.

he quickly outgrew rep'ing someone else's product. "There wasn't anyone that I wanted to ride for and, honestly, no one could afford me," he says half-joking, but in hindsight it was true. So Line teamed with Greg Dileo, who'd originally recruited him to Division 23, and Mike MacEntire of Mack Dawg Films to found Forum Snowboards, which turned out to be more than a snowboard brand; it was a movement at the core level. "It was based on how I became successful, just filming video parts and being a progressive rider: doing the newest things out there, inventing tricks," he says. Under the umbrella of Four Star Distribution, which managed Foursquare, the threesome and their fledgling company packed serious marketing horsepower. At the center of the operation was one of the most popular snowboarders at the time who was renowned for his style, united with the top freestyle filmmaker. Line and MacEntire recruited a team of "young, small-name kids who we saw were gonna be the next step," he says. In 1996, complete with a team of rising talents and a philosophy of having the riders inform product design, Forum Snowboards practically cornered the market on cool.

In 1999, Line completed his coup by winning three Rider's Polls in *TransWorld Snowboarding Magazine*—Favorite All-Around Rider, Best Video Section, and Best Freerider—along with Top 10 Big-Mountain Rider, even though he's not technically a big-mountain rider. He also won two Winter X-Games gold medals in Slopestyle and Big Air the same year. In 2001, the Rider's Poll crowned him "Rock Star of the Year."

"There are some people who come into the sport and then leave," says Tara Dakides, who rides for another Four Star snowboard brand called Jeenyus. "And there are some who come and stay. Peter's one of those people who will always be remembered from generation to generation." **//**

Tara Dakides shifts to fourth and buries the throttle. She's just crested turn nine at Infineon Raceway, a spectacular NASCAR road course nestled in picturesque Sonoma wine country, and she's screaming down the back stretch at more than one hundred miles per hour. The five-time X-Games gold medalist is taking practice laps in an open-wheeled formula race car in preparation for her first race. // Slipping behind the wheel of a race car follows suit for this twenty-eight-year-old Southern California native. Since about 1998, Dakides started to dominate women's slopestyle and big air competitions, and she earned a reputation for going big—really big—and riding with very little fear. As a result, she crossed a threshold in women's snowboarding. "She rides with the same level of confidence and courage as a guy does," says Jake Burton. "Although there have been other women along the way who have done that, it's never been in this sort of technical, freestyle way with rails and big airs. The way she charges is freakin' impressive." Others just state, "She rides like a guy," and that pretty much says it all. // So it comes as no surprise that we find her pulling two Gs as she charges through a sharp hairpin here in Sonoma. In fact, race-car driving always caught her attention, but a lucrative career in snowboarding didn't leave time for much else. A string of injuries with months of rehab and recovery made time. "I was trying to keep myself busy," she says of filling the downtime from two knee surgeries in as many years. "Once I could do things that were low-impact, and I could still get around, I went and did a kart school up in Oxnard, California. It was like a light went on, and I thought, 'Wow, this is something that I would love to do.' After meeting some of the "right

// **OPPOSITE:** Tara and her dog Buddy living the mountain life in Mammoth Lakes, California, 2003.

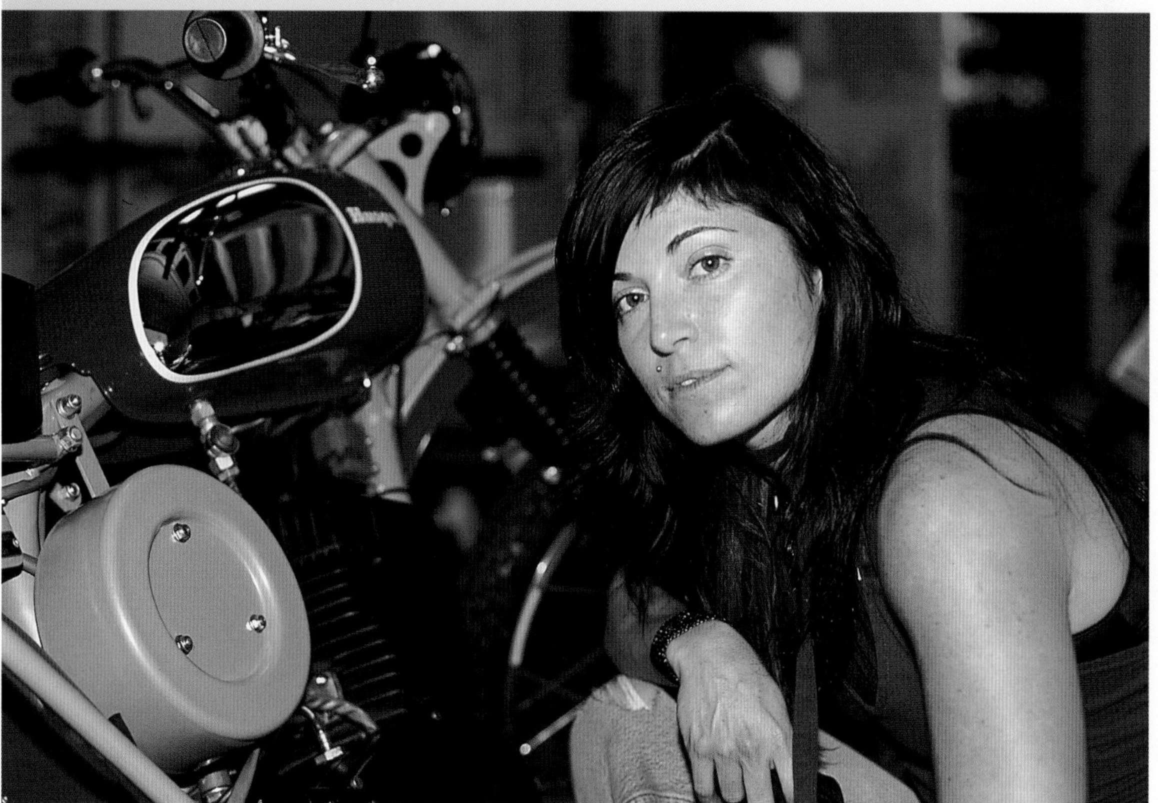

// Car racing and motorcycles: Tara's off-the-hill fix for her need for speed.

people," she was asked to drive in the Baja 1000 in 2003, and that she did—about two hundred miles of hauling ass across the Mexican desert behind the wheel of a custom Baja race car. With a couple advanced driving courses under her belt, including the ESPN Russell Racing Drivers School, she acquired a license to race and got some support from Yokohama tires. Now she's about to compete in her first SCCA Formula Russell Championship race.

After a few more laps, with the practice day winding down, Dakides feels a boost of confidence and starts pushing it harder. It's in her nature to test the limit. At one point, though, she loses control and panics. The wheels lock, sending her careening into a wall. Fortunately, there is Styrofoam to buffer the impact and she's okay. The car has only minor body damage, and barely anyone is around to see it. This wasn't the case just a few months earlier.

In February of 2004, after winning a silver medal in the X-Games slopestyle, Dakides appeared on *The Late Show with David Letterman*. The producers built a massive wooden jump outside the studio in the middle of 53rd Street that was then covered in snow. It was supposed to launch Dakides over a smallish, twenty-foot gap into action-sports-television history. "They'd never had a girl do any kind of stunt or anything like that," she says. "It's only been [skier] Johnny Mosley and [motocrossers] Cary Hart and Travis Pastrana. I think they were excited to bring a female into it." All didn't go as planned.

"A friend of mine was hitting it to try and feel what they needed to do to make it better," she says, "and they just weren't getting it to where it was even a jump that I could clear." Mitigating factors such as a lack of building materials, warm weather melting the snow, and the pressure of a big-time production further eroded her chances of success. "And I was thinking, 'Well, I'm gonna look like an idiot on TV because I'm not going to be able to clear this jump, and people aren't going to understand why,'" she remembers. "So I just basically got through it and I was like, 'Don't worry, we'll figure it out, just build it up.'"

In order for her to get more speed, they built an extension and made the run-in taller. From this teetering viewpoint, she got a perilous view of the street below. It didn't look too forgiving, and the backside 360 she was supposed to do didn't feel right for this jump. "The next thing you know I'm on the air, and Dave's talking, and I'm talking to him," she says, "and as soon as I made a turn, the snow gave away. I mean, afterwards, people were like, 'You should have seen your line, you could see the wood through the snow!' And I just—I got stuck on the wood, and just said, 'Oh, shit,' on the way up the lip." A witness would later report that "she swore so loudly as she was coming down the ramp, probably knowing she wasn't going to make it."

"I knew that I was in for some trouble," she says. Launching off the side of the ramp, out of control, Dakides flew twenty-five feet by most estimates. She took out a cameraman on the way down and fell straight to the asphalt, suffering a concussion, knocking herself unconscious, and tweaking her back.

While Dakides recovered in the ER, a media storm brewed. "[Letterman] cancelled two shows because of what happened. It just spread like wildfire in New York, and I woke up the next day to being on the cover of the [*New York*] *Post*, the *New York Times*, and the *Daily* [*News*]," she says. "Paparazzi were trying to climb on the roof and sneak in through the top of the hospital, through the top floor. Reporters found where my mom lived and where my dad lived and went to their house. It was *crazy*. It was totally surreal."

//

The story of Tara Dakides reads like a Hollywood script. If it were fiction, you might accuse it of being cliché. As an only child, she grew up in Southern California's Laguna Hills, a conservative, middle-class community in the heart of Orange County. The picture-perfect childhood included gymnastics, which "was a heavy focus for many years," she says. Skiing also entered the picture when she was only four years old—family trips to local mountains. "And then I quit gymnastics because of family problems. My parents got divorced. That was, you know, whatever," she says dismissively. As armchair psychologists, we're left to fill in the blanks.

Dakides ended up living with her mom. She satisfied her natural athleticism with soccer, and then discovered skateboarding. "I had a skateboard

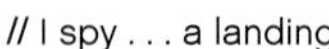

// I spy . . . a landing.

when I was in fifth grade," she remembers, "but I didn't really start skating until about seventh grade, so I was about thirteen." About that same time, she and her mom rented a snowboard "because I had a crash on my skis, so I hated my skis." In her second year of riding, the "troubled teen" immersed herself in the snowboard park. "I was never a good student," she freely admits, "and I always got in trouble. I was definitely a rebellious kid." Of course, at this time, skateboarding and snowboarding were rebellious outlets. "It's one of the reasons why the park was developed," she says. "They wanted us to stay over in one section of the mountain and not intermingle. It was like, 'Okay, you guys stay over there, 'cause we don't understand you.'" Increasingly, neither did her parents. "Nobody was telling me what to do," she says, "so it kind of led my parents to . . . it drove them crazy, basically, so they didn't know what to do with me. So I left school and I left home when I was fifteen, and I moved up to L.A. for a little while."

Subscribing to all things rebellious, Dakides traveled and lived with punk-rock bands. Immersed in the L.A. scene, she indulged herself with tattoos and body piercings. "It was hard," she remembers. "It was definitely a hard way to do things. But, man, it was fun." Fortunately, she avoided the scene's biggest pitfall. "I had a lot of friends in bands who got messed up on drugs and things like that," she says. But deep down she knew this wasn't where she was meant to be. She knew she had a gift and felt a responsibility to honor it. So at sixteen years old, she sold her stereo for $300 and bought a Greyhound ticket to Mammoth "with one phone number of a guy that I barely knew," she says. "I moved up there with, like, everything that I had basically hanging off of me." One of those things was, of course, her snowboard.

Dakides found a new home in the Eastern Sierras, eking out a meager existence as a snowboard bum. Pursuing a career in snowboarding by riding hard and promoting herself to the industry at trade shows and through "sponsor-me" videos, she worked only as much as it took to support the habit. For a resourceful eighteen-year-old, that wasn't much. "I got fired from all my jobs," she told ESPN's Dan Patrick. "I worked at an Ace Hardware as a cashier and got fired because I showed up with my lip pierced with a safety pin. And I got fired from a gourmet sausage place because I wanted to make a snowboard contest and my boss wouldn't give me the days off, so I just didn't show up."

With a background in both gymnastics and skateboarding in combination with a punk-rock attitude, Dakides funneled her raw talent into an impressive, go-for-broke riding style. "Her snowboarding is not dainty," says Peter Line. "She does stuff that I won't do." Riding rails and picnic tables in the wake of snowboarding's new-school revolution, she was a pioneer of women's jib. Sponsors took notice. In 1994, she turned pro and hasn't been fired from a job since.

//

Cut to the 2004 Winter X-Games in Aspen, Colorado. Dakides stands atop the slopestyle course ready to take her run. She's barely slept. Instead, she's been obsessing about her line and how the competition had stepped it up in the last couple years. It won't be enough to do a backflip and a backside 360 to win. Things have changed. Girls are throwing down 540s and switch tricks and frontside boardslides—upping the bar that she'd been setting for the past ten years. The pressure for her to do well, especially at the X-Games, is tremendous.

Two years ago, she won the gold here, and it's been a rollercoaster of crashes and recovery ever since. While practicing on a rail that same season, she slipped and caught her board underneath it, slamming her leg against one of the supporting posts. For many, it would've been a career-ending injury—a broken fibula, torn ACL, nerve damage to her toes, and a concussion that took fifteen stitches to mend. The Terrorizer, as she's known, spent fourteen days in the hospital.

Upon her return to the snow nine months later, following a questionable rehab procedure whereby the ACL grows back on its own rather than replacing it, Dakides "hit a twenty-foot kicker, came up a little short, and re-tore the sucker," she says. Despite reinjuring the knee, she still wanted to compete at the X-Games. She hired a personal trainer and braced up the knee for battle. But it didn't hold. "When I came home from the X-Games, I went under the knife again," she says.

Now, after almost two full seasons off, she's making a comeback of sorts. And it's not gone unnoticed. As she stands here, ready to drop in, the cover of *FHM*, a popular men's magazine, features Dakides clad only in body paint. She's naked, save for a few brush strokes and a massive tattoo extending half-way up her back. This is the other, ahem, side of Tara Dakides. Though she may ride (and cuss and spit) like a guy on the snow, that's where it ends. There's no question, she's sexy with a capital X. Indeed, her unique combination of skill and sex appeal helped to cross yet another threshold—that of mainstream pop culture. After appearing on its cover, *FHM* readers voted Dakides one of the "Top 100 Sexiest Women in the World." She secured a respectable ninetieth on the list, while Brittney Spears won the top spot. In years past, she turned up in *Maxim* and *Rolling Stone* magazines and once graced the cover of *Sport Illustrated Women*. Dakides (pronounced with a long E) was on the way to becoming a household name.

Into her run, she butt-checks off a rail in the upper section and then stomps an impressive backside 720, a trick she hasn't done in nearly three years—one few woman can do at all. She's stoked about her run. It feels like a weight's been lifted. She feels like getting back to riding.

Looking back on the moment of her second ACL injury, she remembers looking toward the season

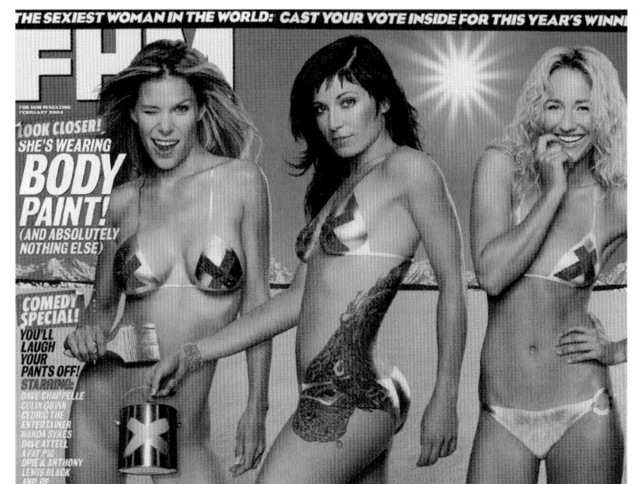

// **CLOCKWISE FROM LEFT:** Tara's fans at a contest showing no restraint. // Dakides on the cover of *FHM* (center) modeling little more than some carefully placed brush strokes in 2004. // This guy has taken an X-Game autograph signing to another level.

// **OPPOSITE:** Inverted and totally in control off a kicker. // **ABOVE:** Rounding out the freestyle trifecta in the halfpipe. // **LEFT:** Backside rail-slide in the park.

// Dakides, ruler of her universe.

and "to my other goals like having a video part and an interview in the magazines and not forgetting the industry and where I came from," she says, "because I had been caught up in so much mainstream stuff." The Letterman incident put snowboarding on hold for another three months and only catapulted her further into the mainstream, for better or worse. ***//***

These days you're more likely to find Dakides listening to Norah Jones at her mountain home in Mammoth Lakes or her beach house in Oceanside than, say, Minor Threat in a Venice Beach nightclub. She, along with professional snowboarding, has made a transition from what she calls the "punk rock years" to its present state, which carries certain responsibilities. "I try and be forward, allowing it to go into the mainstream but also where I think it still remains cool," she says. Her recent Campbell's Soup commercial is a prime example. She describes how they wanted her backflipping with a can of soup in her hand. "And I'm like, 'I'm not gonna do that, it's gay.'"

You're also just as likely to find her on primetime TV holding a microphone as you are on ESPN sliding down a rail. In the summer of 2004, Dakides started hosting a show called *The Menu* on Fox. "It's movies, music, fashion, TV, and action sports," she says. Overall, though, being a TV personality isn't where she wants to be. Besides not wanting to have her hair and makeup done so often, "it takes me away from other fun things that I like to do," she says. Like, for instance, driving race cars.

Dakides finished that first race in Sonoma with a respectable fifth place. You can bet that if she wants to take it to the next level, she will. She'll push the envelope of women's driving just as she's done with snowboarding, and the story will offer inspiration.

"I remember when I was younger, reading stories and interviews about people that I looked up to in some way," she says, "and whenever I could find some story that I could relate to, about somebody that made it and got through it, then there was hope. That's where the inspiration came from, and that's what helped me get through some of my tough times."

Fade to black. ***//***

"Is that Shaun White?" a young fan asks excitedly from behind the banners of the 2004 U.S. Open halfpipe event. His dad doesn't think so. There is one sure way to pick one of the world's top riders, seventeen-year-old Shaun White, out of the lineup. You can look up, as he launches fifteen feet out of the pipe, and spy the graphic of his signature board. If it's not blurred by a 1080-degree spin, and you can make out the "SW" with an evil-looking bunny graphic, you know it's the one and only. You know it's the prodigy-turned-snowboarding-superstar. You know it's Shaun White. // In fact, Shaun is the guy with the mask tucked snuggly under his Oakley goggles like a futuristic gunslinger, totally covering his young, freckled face. He also wears signature Shaun White boots and a signature Shaun White helmet—so you can't make out his floppy, scarlet locks—as he gets ready to drop in for his first qualifying run. // It's been an okay year so far for the Burton Global Team rider. He racked up a string of big first-place finishes at the Innsbruck Air & Style contest in Austria, the Sessions-at-Vail slopestyle and rail jam events, and the Winter X-Games slopestyle in Aspen, Colorado. However, he had "some technical difficulties with his knee" in the X-Games halfpipe and couldn't finish. A small meniscus tear lead to surgery and six weeks of rehab and recovery. Now he's ready to compete again—to go back to work. // White drops into the monstrous, alpine wave—complete with fifteen-foot walls—as if he's done this all his life. Of course, that's because he has. The five-foot-four enigma started riding when he was six, started hitting (and landing) jumps on his second day, and turned pro when he was twelve, at this very event. Five years later, White is a podium favorite. He goes huge on the first hit, setting himself up for

// **OPPOSITE:** Who was that masked man? White cruises through qualifiers at the 2004 U.S. Open in Stratton, Vermont.

Mountain Dew

a spectacular series of ultra-smooth and pin-point-accurate tricks. Most of his rivals can do them, too, but White's seamless and seemingly effortless flow from launching to tweaking and landing—all in one motion—sets him apart. Maybe it's because he started so young or because he's also a pro skate-boarder. Maybe it's because he was born in the right place at the right time or because he hangs around with Tony Hawk. Or maybe he just loves it enough to be this good.

//

Roger and Cathy White give birth to their second son, Shaun, in San Diego, California, in the fall of 1986. Meanwhile, the World Snowboarding Champion-ships has just moved from Soda Springs to Brecken-ridge, Colorado. Metal edges have become the standard in snowboard manufacturing, and Stratton Mountain is offering the first organized snowboarding instruction. As Shaun White is taking his first breaths, the sport is fully happening. And very few pros who ride at White's level today can say the same. Snowboarding hit a turning point in 1985, and there's something to be said for entering this world after that point. If timing is everything, then Roger and Cathy nailed it.

Growing up in the SoCal surf–skate scene pro-vided the ideal breeding ground for a would-be board-sports superstar. Young White took to skate-boarding not long after he could walk, and started skiing shortly thereafter. "Then my brother [Jesse] started snowboarding," he says, "and I was, like, 'I gotta snowboard.'" He tried it, loved it, but couldn't find a board his size. "My mom ended up calling Burton and was like, 'Hey, you know, my son's trying snowboarding, so do you have a little board?' And they were, like, 'That's crazy because we're starting our kids' line." With timing on their side once again, White landed a board sponsor in Burton, and he's been loyal to the company ever since.

// **LEFT:** The future face of snowboarding . . . several years ago. // **OPPOSITE:** Suspended above the pipe in Mount Hood in 1999.

The combination of undeniable talent and a supportive, tight-knit family set the stage for snow-boarding's first child star. Each weekend during the winter his parents would drive three hours each way to the ski areas near Big Bear Lake, California. "I'd go up there and learn like five new tricks and come back down," he says. "And every time I was just more and more excited about snowboarding."

// OPPOSITE: Señor Blanco grabbing some mute under the lights of a Big Air comp in 2001.

His mother lobbied sponsors at the trade shows and managed his young career, gaining a reputation as snowboarding's premier stage mom. In the summer, the family headed north to Mount Hood in Oregon for snowboarding camp on the glacier. A Standard Films cinematographer, Rich Van Everett, discovered White and asked if he could shoot him. "So I went over to my mom," White says, "and I'm all, 'Mom, this guy wants to film me.' And she's like, 'I'd better go talk to him.' So she introduced herself, and we ended up shooting a bunch." In addition to dominating junior competitions at age seven, he started showing up in snowboarding's top films.

At the U.S. Open, a year after he'd won the amateur overall championship, Shaun realized something needed to change for him in order to progress with snowboarding. "I was questioning what I was doing at that point," he remembers. "I was winning with the same run. It wasn't making me better, and that's what I wanted. I wanted to ride with better guys and get better." At twelve years old, he entered the pro halfpipe competition but didn't qualify. The next day, he tried to enter the juniors, "and all the parents were pissed," he says. "It got really heavy, I mean, having someone else's mom giving me dirty looks. I'm just like, 'Uh . . . I'm twelve.' Yeah, it was weird."

//

Alas, the prodigy joined the pro ranks, and it paid. He entered the Vans Triple Crown and Grand Prix events, competing against the best the world had to offer and elevating his game in the process. "It was a year of mostly watching," he says. "I watched Ross's [Powers] run, and I was like, 'Okay, he's doing these tricks and that. I looked at my tricks and knew what I needed to do.'" He placed in the top ten throughout 2000, and by the time Terje Haakonsen's Arctic Challenge came around in the spring of 2001, he found himself at the top of the podium in snowboarding's most respected event, capturing his first big halfpipe victory.

Being pegged as the prodigy, though, has its share of drawbacks. "This one year [2002] I had two firsts and, like, thirteen seconds," he says, emphasizing the frustration. "You can take a couple seconds here and there, that's cool, but there were some events where I was like, 'Aw man, I know I had a better run.' And I just felt like the judges were like, 'Okay, here's a second.' I wanted to get a third, you know, just to mix it up."

This stigma (and aggravation) spilled over into the 2002 Olympic qualifiers. "I ended up losing by three-tenths of a point to J.J. [Thomas]," he says. "I wasn't upset or anything, but the worst was dropping into the halfpipe with the announcer saying, 'He's probably not gonna make it this year, but he's got a lot of time.' And I'm like, 'No, I'll make it this time!'" Settling for an alternate position on the team, White shrugged it off with an "all good" attitude. It was the last year he battled with perceptions as the prodigious up-and-comer.

After losing the 2002 X-Games halfpipe to Todd Richards, who "totally swiped it" on his last run,

// The undisputed king of slopestyle throws a picture-perfect frontside boardslide to 360 in 2003. He was just a kid then.

Shaun said to himself, "You know what, I'm gonna win this thing when I come back." Calling his shot, the determined sixteen-year-old showed up the next go-round in Aspen, Colorado, in January of 2003 and cleaned up—gold medals in both the halfpipe *and* slopestyle events. This unique brand of dominance, combined with his youthful appeal, immediately turned Shaun White into a major action-sports commodity. Sponsors flocked to invest in Shaun White, Inc. Then, to raise the bar another notch, he went ahead and turned pro in skateboarding.

When he wasn't traveling and snowboarding and competing throughout his adolescence, White rode his skateboard at home "strictly for fun." He grew up in the beach community of Carlsbad, California, which is also the birthplace and home of skateboard legend Tony Hawk, so it's no coincidence that Hawk discovered the young talent. White started touring with Hawk's famous Boom-Boom Huck Jam demo tour during the summer when he was only thirteen. Though not a pro and not competing, he'd successfully crossed over between board sports like no one else in history.

In 2003, White transitioned from "for fun" to "for real" when he turned pro at the Slam City Jam in Vancouver, Canada. The rookie pro snatched a fourth in vert, earning him a shot at the Summer X-Games. Placing a respectable sixth there in the same event, he became the first action-sports athlete to compete in unique events at both the Winter and Summer X-Games, which lead to an ESPN ESPY award for Best Action Sports Athlete of the Year. Certainly, many snowboarders skate, and a handful (including White) surf, mostly for fun and to complement their riding. But by pushing the envelope in both snowboarding and skateboarding, White established himself as an action-sport figure who is beyond compare.

//

There are actually two Shaun Whites. One is a superstar around whom so much hype and money and media revolve. The other is a down-to-earth kid who still lives with his parents, his older brother, and his younger sister. He goes to high school and has friends his own age. Most of them don't snowboard, and they rarely discuss it. He can even be shy. This is the Shaun White with whom very few are familiar. But while this Shaun White might play the *Cool Boarders 4* video game with his friends, the other Shaun White is actually a character *in* the video game.

The other Shaun White bought the house his family lives in, together with several others as investments that his mother manages. He won several cars in snowboard competitions before his sixteenth birthday and still went out and bought one when he got his license. He has criss-crossed the world countless times. *USA Today* and *Sports Illustrated* published feature stories about this Shaun White, the same one who's shown up on

// High-flying in Hemsdel, Norway, 2002.

// **OPPOSITE:** Enough amplitude at the 2001 Arctic Challenge to walk away with Big Air gold. // **BELOW:** The pinnacle of competitive jibbing in 2002.

Live with Regis and Kelly and two MTV shows, *Total Request Live* and *MTV Cribs*. When this Shaun White turned sixteen, he went to an Ozzfest concert and got a suprising taste of what being a recognized star can bring. "This guy comes up to me and says, 'Hey, you're Shaun White,'" he told *Snowboarder* magazine. "So I'm like, 'Yeah, nice to meet ya.' Just then he grabs his girlfriend, and all of sudden she lifts up her shirt and flashes me." This fanatical behavior also manifests itself in a number of dedicated, unofficial Shaun White websites, in addition to the official one, which his brother maintains. And in 2004 he starred in *The White Album*, a snowboard/skateboard movie from Cinema Seone about . . . Shaun White.

In addition to endemic sponsorships from Burton, Oakley, and Volcom, White endorses Mountain Dew, Sony Playstation, and Target, appearing in television commercials and sporting their logos. "Target wants to sponsor anything I do," he told *Snowboarder*, describing how the first-of-its-kind relationship works. "They're just like, 'What can we do for you? We want to be a part of what you're doing.' I get to pick an event, and they're going to sponsor the rider's lounge—make it the sickest lounge ever. Bring in chefs, big couches—everyone walking around in slippers. It's gonna be sick."

Dubbing him the next Terje Haakonsen or Tony Hawk might be flattering. It certainly makes great copy, but then again it might also be an understatement or at the very least inaccurate. Haakonsen and Hawk did amazing things for their sports, which went largely unnoticed in the mainstream until recently. White's unique skill set, his timing, and his appeal are conspiring to revolutionize the acceptance and perception of both snowboarding and skateboarding. Sponsors are, for the first time, using a snowboarder—an individual—to boost their image and market products to a general audience.

White's greatness is defined as much by what he's already done as by what he's yet to do. Undoubtedly, his greatest accomplishments lay ahead, and that's saying a lot. As for the immediate, he just wants to keep getting better, "keep doing what I've been doing for these past few years," he says. Assuming he does, it will lead to the Olympics in 2006, a gold medal, and even greater hero status among snowboarders, skateboarders, and the American public. In the meantime, it's a wait-and-see approach, one that's best done looking up from the edge of a halfpipe. **//**

// OPPOSITE: Breakfast of champions, 2002.

>THE WAY OF THE SNOWBOARDER

Mountains make up one-fifth of the land surface of the Earth. Standing as metaphoric monuments on the grandest of scales, they have captivated the collective spirit and imagination of humankind since the beginning of time. In religion, they are the conduits through which prophets receive Holy Scripture, the place where mortals come to connect with the divine. In ancient myths, they hosted the gods as inhabitants. Storied peaks have played pivotal roles in human conquest, and in turn, have shaped civilizations. According to *Mountains, The Illustrated Library of the Earth,* these towering land masses are vital to the well-being of more than half the population of the world. Mountains of the snow-covered variety are vital to the way of the snowboarder.

From the rolling hills of the Midwest to mighty Mount Everest at 29,500 feet, any slope is fair game if it's covered in snow. Most practitioners of the sport prefer ski areas with their high-speed chair lifts, warm base lodges, and manicured slopes. There are a handful of the larger areas—fantastic resort destinations like Whistler Blackcomb and Jackson Hole in North America or Chamonix and St. Anton in Europe—that could be considered snowboarding's great cathedrals. They are places of pilgrimage, where likeminded devotees from all over the world congregate during the holy season of winter. The few who feel a larger calling, so to speak, venture into the backcountry.

The term "backcountry" evokes both a state of mind and a physical space. It exists naturally—wildly—on all continents and is afforded the utmost respect for its volatile beauty. No matter how one accesses the backcountry, be it by helicopter, snowmobile, or a long hike, the journey inevitably culminates in a cathartic descent down a mountainside covered in the snowy white stuff that dreams are made of.

It's the fresh snow that echoes a most intense and irresistible siren song. Powder begets joy and speed and flight. To surf powder is to exist in a state somewhere between weightlessness and suspended animation, a Twilight Zone where boundaries are only in one's perception.

The act of snowboarding compels the human spirit, tapping into a visceral sense of adventure. For the devoted it symbolizes freedom—the same boundless range of motion that birds take for granted. Transcending the rigors of daily life, snowboarding can open doors into the psyche that may have otherwise remained locked. For a select few, it is a career and lifestyle filled with fame and drama, creativity and pride. For most, it is a departure and well-earned escape from whatever happens Monday through Friday. For each of us, snowboarding is the way. ***//***

// **OPPOSITE:** Turns? Those just slow you down. Valdez, Alaska. // **FOLLOWING PAGES:** Sunset on the Aiguille, which flank Mont Blanc in Chamonix, France. // Gigi Ruff launches one more before the Norwegian sun dips behind the Arctic mountains.

ART CENTER
COLLEGE LIBRARY

INDEX

Numbers in *italics* refer to illustrations.

PHOTOGRAPH CREDITS

© Arbor Snowboards: 22
Mike Basich: 82, 83, 87 top
Bo Bridges: 162, 165 left, 166, 167, 168
© Burton Snowboards: 11, 15, 16 top, 17, 21
Chris Carnel: 78, 85 left, 110
Jim Cassimus: 33 top, 36–37
Aaron Chang: 67, 69, 74–75, 108
Jeff Curtes: 2–3, 4, 12, 19, 20, 23, 49, 64–65, 81, 93 top, 94 top and bottom, 113 top and bottom, 123, 124, 127, 130, 131, 134, 139, 142, 143, 144 sequence, 173, 176–77, 179, 180, 181, 183, 185, 188–89
Bud Fawcett: 16 bottom, 18, 34–35, 39, 42–43, 44–45, 46–47, 51 right, 52 right, 54, 55, 56, 57, 70, 71, 73, 80, 85 right, 92, 99 all, 100, 101 all, 102, 103, 106, 107, 108, 107 all, 132, 133, 134, 140, 141
Susie Floros: 159, 160, 165
© Forum: 147, 156, 157
Mark Gallup: 58, 60, 89, 90, 97, 136–37, 138, 149, 150, 152–53, 155, 172, 174
Mike Hatchett: 121
Rob Reed: 129, 171, 186–87
Patrick Reeves: 93 bottom
Patty Sagovia: 87 bottom
Adam Sedway: 115, 117 top, 118–19, 120
© Tom Sims: 24, 27, 29, 30, 33 bottom, 40, 51 left, 52 left, 104
Vincent Skoglund: front cover
© Standard Films: 117 bottom
© Winterstick: 8–9
Hiro Yamada: 63

PROJECT MANAGER: **DEBORAH AARONSON**
EDITOR: **SAMANTHA TOPOL**
DESIGNER: **BRANKICA KOVRLIJA**
DESIGN ASSISTANCE: **SHAWN DAHL**
PRODUCTION MANAGER: **NORMAN WATKINS**

LIBRARY OF CONGRESS CATALOGING-IN-PUBLICATION DATA
Reed, Rob.
The way of the snowboarder / Rob Reed.
p. cm.
Includes bibliographical references and index.
ISBN 0-8109-5939-9 (alk. paper)
1. Snowboarding. I. Title.
GV857.S57R43 2005
796.93--dc22
2005005861

Copyright © 2005 Rob Reed

Published in 2005 by Harry N. Abrams, Incorporated, New York
All rights reserved. No part of the contents of this book may be reproduced without the written permission of the publisher.

Printed and bound in China
10 9 8 7 6 5 4 3 2 1

HARRY N. ABRAMS, INC.
100 Fifth Avenue
New York, N.Y. 10011
www.abramsbooks.com

Abrams is a subsidiary of

ACKNOWLEDGEMENTS

For Kristen

In memory of Craig Kelly. Without you, who knows where we'd be.

Thanks to all of the people involved in making this book possible: My good friend and attorney Peter Salaverry; my tireless editor Samantha Topol; the interviewees: Jake Burton, Tom Sims, Tom Burt, Tina Basich, Mike Hatchett, Terje Haakonsen, Peter Line, Tara Dakides, and Shaun White; my assistant editor Meghan McCarthy; Caroline Andrew and Sandy Yusen at Burton; Sean Dog, Out of Bounds Adventures, and the Captain's Choice Motel in Haines, Alaska; Jeff and Paula Pensiero and John Buffrey at the Baldface Lodge in Nelson, B.C.; Cris Whittaker at The Familie; Tom Hsieh, Aaron Chang, Bo Bridges, Mike Basich, Bob Carlson, Chris Jensen, and Dan McNamara.

Special thanks to Burton Snowboards, Salomon Snowboards, Chris Carnel, Jeff Curtes, Bud Fawcett, Mark Gallup, and Tom Sims for their superb imagery.

To all of those who've inspired and supported my work over the years: Rob Story, John Bresee, Keith Carlson, David Reddick, Derrick Taylor, Mark North, Chris Guibert, Ben Court, Grant Davis, Stephanie Pearson, Matt Schneiderman, Dave Kenny, Peter Kray, Colin Helms, Les Shu, Nancy Coulter Parker, Doug Schnitzspahn, Mark Langton, Pat Hom and Nissan, Joani Lynch and Mammoth Mountain Ski Resort.

For my family and friends: Mom and Dad; Sheila and Bob; Jenn, Mike, Pam, and Justin; Nicole, Sandy, Ava, Camille, Sarah, Ryan, Michal, and Dave; Jamie, EJ, Campbell, Josh, Jason, Teddy, Steve, Ron, Dorothy, and Joe.

Front cover: David Benedek, backside boardslide, Chapelco, Argentina, 2001.
Back cover: Tom Burt, Alaska, 1997.